Lessons Learned

*An Open Letter to Recreational Therapy
Students and Practitioners*

David R. Austin, Ph.D.
Professor Emeritus
Indiana University

SAGAMORE
PUBLISHING

Publishers: Joseph J. Bannon/Peter Bannon
VP of Sales and Marketing: M. Douglas Sanders
Director of Development and Production: Susan M. Davis
Cover and Interior Design: Susan M. Davis

Library of Congress Catalog Card Number: 2010933977
ISBN: 978-1-57167- 582-8
Printed in the United States.

10 9 8 7 6 5 4 3

Sagamore Publishing, LLC
www.sagamorepub.com
1807 N Federal Drive
Urbana, IL 61801-1051

I dedicate this book to all who have taught me what I know about the phenomenal profession of recreational therapy. I have been extremely blessed to have had wonderful colleagues, professors, students, and clients from whom I have learned many lessons.

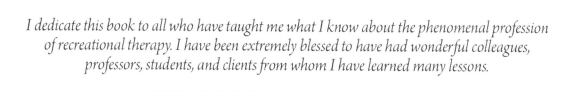

Contents

Acknowledgments   viii
Preface   ix

Lesson

Understanding Recreational Therapy
1   Recreational Therapy is a Lot More than Diversion!   1
2   Our Mission Includes Health Promotion   4
3   What Makes RT Therapeutic?   6
4   Do You Know Who We Are?   8
5   Recreational Therapists Need a Philosophy of Practice   12
6   The Importance of Recreation and Leisure   15

Approaches to Recreational Therapy
7   Recreational Therapists Use a Strength-Based Approach   17
8   Client Strengths Include Traits and Resources   19
9   Recreational Therapy is Action Oriented, but the Emphasis
    is on the Client and Not on the Activity   21
10 Recreation and Leisure Activities Provide Fun with a Purpose   22
11 The Therapeutic Relationship is at the Heart of Recreational Therapy   24
12 Recreational Therapy Offers a Unique, Caring Atmosphere   26
13 Recreational Therapy is Customized Care   28
14 Recreational Therapy as a Dress Rehearsal for Life   30

Conceptual Foundations for Recreational Therapy
15 The WHO Definition of Health and Its Acceptance
    by Recreational Therapists   31
16 Carl Rogers: The Grandfather of Recreational Therapy   33
17 Positive Psychology and Recreational Therapy   35
18 Freud and Skinner Weren't Completely Wrong   38

Working With Groups
19 The New Recreational Therapist's Anxiety in Group Leadership   40
20 Recreational Therapy Groups Offer Participants Numerous Benefits   41
21 Group Processing Should Be Regularly Completed with RT Groups   43
22 Techniques When Clients Don't Participate in Group Discussions   45
23 Get a Background in Group Dynamics, Because You'll Need It   46

The Recreational Therapist

24	Recreational Therapists are Models for Clients	48
25	Is Recreational Therapy an Art or a Science, or Both?	49
26	Enthusiasm	51
27	Extroversion	53
28	Dare to Share	55
29	Learn to Relax	56
30	Value Values	58
31	Gaining Cultural Competence	60
32	Maintaining Confidentiality	62
33	Burnout	64
34	Why Clients Like RTs: The Norm of Reciprocity	66
35	Clinical Supervision	68
36	Self-Awareness	70
37	Being a Team Player	72
38	Being Professional	74
39	Being an Advocate for Our Profession	77

Techniques for Recreational Therapists

40	Learning by Doing	79
41	It's Good to Give Feedback	80
42	When Clients Change	82
43	Engage Your Clients	85
44	Aggression Begets Aggression	86
45	Use Self-Disclosure Sparingly and in a Timely Fashion	88
46	Be Supportive of Clients	90
47	The Use of Gimmicks Can Be Good	92
48	Employ and Foster Intrinsic Motivation	94
49	Here and Now	96
50	Build Self-Esteem	98
51	Leisure Counseling	101
52	Activities Spur Conversation	103
53	Use Touch Therapeutically	104
54	Therapeutic Recreation Skills Are Not Esoteric	105
55	My Favorite Approaches to Effective Listening	107
56	Top Teaching Principles	109

Social Psychology and Recreational Therapy

57	Recreational Therapists as Applied Social Psychologists	111
58	The Overjustification Effect	113
59	Self-Efficacy: Why Some Clients Try and Others Don't	115

60	Social Facilitation	117
61	Self-Handicapping	119
62	Self-Fulfilling Prophecy	121
63	Learned Helplessness	123

What to Do and Not Do as an RT

64	Evidence-Based Practice: A Concept RT Should Embrace	125
65	Say "Yes" to RT Research	128
66	Never Become Sexual with Clients	130
67	Never Become Anti-Intellectual	131
68	(Almost) Never Make Choices for Clients	132
69	Cherish the Opportunity to Do Recreational Therapy	133

| *References* | 134 |
| *About the Author* | 137 |

Acknowledgments

I would be remiss if I did not acknowledge those individuals who read all or parts of earlier drafts of my book and who have provided me with insightful feedback. Heartfelt thanks to Drs. Victoria Dawn Shelar, Marieke Van Puymbroeck, and Jerry Kelley, whose comments and suggestions have made this a better book. Also, special thanks to Susan Davis and Doug Sanders at Sagamore Publishing LLC for their support in putting together the book you have in your hands now. Finally, I would like to express my sincere appreciation to Joe and Peter Bannon, of Sagamore Publishing LLC, for believing in my book and publishing it so that it is available to both students and practitioners.

Preface

Some of my best ideas have come from other people! That is certainly true for this book.

The inspiration for this book grew out of the enthusiastic responses I received from Canadian and American recreational therapists to two keynote addresses I delivered in 2008. The talks were titled, "This I Believe About Recreational Therapy." During my presentations, I was able to relate to others in my profession of recreational therapy the core beliefs I had developed over the course of 40 some years in the field.

Those talks allowed me to put forth twelve core beliefs I held about recreational therapy. I knew that I would enjoy sharing my most cherished beliefs about recreational therapy, but I wasn't prepared for what happened next. Following my presentations, those that heard my thoughts were really stimulated by what I had to say. Many related their reactions to me. Most agreed with my beliefs, but several were able to debate some of the points I had made. Receiving this reaction to my presentations made me to wonder how I could get my message out to an even larger audience of the recreational therapy professionals.

About that time, I happened across a book by Irvin Yalom, M.D. Yalom, a noted psychotherapist, had written a book titled *The Gift of Therapy: An Open Letter to a New Generation of Therapists and Their Patients*. In this book, Yalom shared insights he had gained over his career with the intent of passing on those insights to a new generation of psychotherapists.

I quickly bought Yalom's book and read it cover to cover. His approach was fascinating. Born from a concern for the future of training in clinical psychology, Yalom's book offered thoughts gained throughout his life on virtually every aspect of psychotherapy.

Yalom mentions in his book that while he never consciously attempted to offer tips to psychotherapists on how to practice, he had in fact done so. The book is filled with advice gained from Yalom's 45 years of clinical practice.

The unique format Yalom used in presenting his ideas made for a book that was easy to read and very digestible. His format of using short chapters filled with examples and few citations was one that I have attempted to emulate in this book. Hopefully readers will find my book to be as easily consumable as Yalom's book.

Yalom's approach in writing his book would provide a model for me as he simply wrote down ideas to share and then took what he believed to be the best of those to use in his book. I used a similar but not identical approach with this book.

I began by jotting down ideas as they came to me, and as I did, I attempted to recall specific instances that illustrated these concepts or ideas. In addition, I went back over my notes for the "This I Believe" presentations for concepts I thought should be included in my book. Finally, I completed what I would have to admit was a rather unsystematic review of the literature I had authored over the years. As

I went, I tossed aside those things that really didn't seem to merit coverage in my book and tried to keep those that I thought would resonate with readers.

All in all, I am pleased with the result. I think my book will, for recreational therapy, accomplish much of what Yalom has for psychotherapy. It gives tips, advice, and raises issues that hopefully will help to guide practice in recreational therapy in years ahead.

The profession of recreational therapy has been very good to me. It has provided me a passion, as well as a living. I truly cherish the years I have had in my beloved profession and I would like to see it continue to grow and prosper.

Perhaps the greatest gift one generation can give to the next is what that generation gained from its experience. As someone who has been identified as a "pioneer" in recreational therapy, I think I am in a unique position to share what I have learned over many years. I present this book with the hope the next generations of recreational therapists will find what I have learned useful to them.

—**David R. Austin, Ph.D., FALS, FDRT**

Recreational Therapy is a Lot More than Diversion!

When I started my career as a recreational therapist, I believed the aim of recreational therapy was helping the psychiatric patients at the hospital where I worked to enjoy themselves through their participation in recreational activities. Such activities had the therapeutic benefit of diverting them from their mental illnesses.

There was nothing "wrong" with this, because all human beings need to escape our problems and concerns from time to time. And recreation activities are one means of diverting ourselves.

Providing diversion is a valid aim recreational therapists may have in helping their clients. Yet, while diversion may be helpful, most recreational therapists dislike being thought of as "diversional therapists."

This is because many times colleagues from other allied health disciplines have attempted to portray recreational therapists as doing nothing but supplying clients with diversions from their problems. Of course, a designation as a diversional therapist implies a lack of clinical intent and expertise on the part of recreational therapists that is demeaning to them. This designation unjustly places recreational therapists on a low level as health care professionals. Through the years, recreational therapists have had to defend themselves from the unfair charge that they offer nothing more than diversion for clients.

This charge that recreational therapy is strictly diversional is unjust from many perspectives. First, recreation as a diversion is not purely escapism. As has already been stated, clients' diversion from their problems can be positive because spending a great deal of their time going over and over their problems is not therapeutic. All of us need time away from the stressors in our lives, and recreation can provide this relief.

Second, and more important in my mind, is that the positive emotions (e.g., enjoyment, fun, feelings of accomplishment) gained from recreation participation lead to far more than diversion or a "feel-good" experience.

Positive emotions can counteract lingering negative emotions. They can ward off negative emotions. Experiencing positive emotions from recreation participation also opens doors for change.

When individuals experience positive emotions, they begin to loosen up, to feel free or less encumbered. They open themselves up so they are more receptive to new thoughts and behaviors. They are far more prone to stretch themselves and to try new experiences that they might avoid if they were not feeling happy or being in a good mood. Think about yourself; are you more open to try new things if you are in a positive, optimistic frame of mind? Of course you are. So are clients.

In fact, a psychologist has constructed a theory to explain the phenomenon of positive emotions producing optimistic actions. The notion that positive emotions broaden people's perspectives and open them to new experiences in which they can build their skills has been formally expressed by Fredrickson (2001) in her book, *Broaden and Build Theory of Positive Emotion.*

Thus, the claim that recreational therapy is solely diversional simply is not true (and besides we know that diversion is not necessarily a bad thing for clients). Recreation participation can and does create positive emotions. In turn, experiencing positive emotions negates negative emotions and opens clients up to risk entering into new experiences. Entering into new experiences can have great therapeutic value by providing opportunities for producing therapeutic change in clients.

At one point in my career as a recreational therapist, I saw my task primarily as applying treatments to remove the symptoms suffered by the psychiatric patients who I served. If someone suffered from anxiety, I attempted to make him less anxious. If a patient were depressed, I tried to get her out of depression.

Again, as with diversion, there was nothing "wrong" with seeking to reduce the symptoms of patients. It is painful to suffer from anxiety or depression so, as a therapist, I should have done anything I could do to help patients gain relief from these negative feelings. For example, patients might find that jogging relaxed them and helped them to feel less anxious so I would assist them to set up a jogging routine. Or for those suffering from depression, I might suggest almost any activity I could engage them in just to get them active and out of their doldrums.

The approach to the patients' total treatment program was diverse and holistic. My recreational therapy interventions were seen as one means for clients to reduce their symptoms. Doctors prescribed drugs to reduce clients' psychiatric symptoms, and I provided activities that helped my clients with symptom reduction. Being focused on treatment gave me a sense of being a part of the treatment team and a real purpose for what I did as a recreational therapist.

But as we go through life, new insights often reveal themselves to us. While it took me a while to realize it, before long I discovered that as a recreational therapist I could help clients beyond just providing symptom reduction. I could do more, much more.

Specifically, once obstacles to health were identified, I could help my clients build traits and abilities that would prepare them to remove or overcome these barriers and then to deal with future life challenges as they encountered them.

I guess you could term this to be rehabilitation (to rebuild traits and abilities) or habilitation (to build traits and abilities). But, in my mind, the terms rehabilitation and habilitation carry medical connotations. What I discovered was rather than concentrating exclusively on medical aspects and client pathology, recreational therapy could also focus on the positive aspects of our clients.

We, in recreational therapy, can alleviate distress by helping our clients gain relief from their symptoms, but additionally we can go far beyond this, helping clients to develop and use their strengths and potentials to deal with barriers to health and to facilitate optimal functioning. We cannot only help our clients to become well again, we can help them to become better than they were before they came to us.

The central element in this approach is focusing on the positive or what is right with the client, rather than on the pathology or disability. The particular pathology or disability represents only one small part of our clients. Our clients are made up of much more. Many positives are to be found in the "intact part" of our clients. Emphasis on the positive by building on client strengths (i.e., traits and abilities) creates a sense of optimism because all people possess strengths that they can develop and use to remove or overcome barriers to health and to promote wellness.

This strengths-based approach provides clients with means to meet barriers that have gotten in the way of the attainment of positive health (which I believe is experienced when barriers to self-actualization are removed). This is what I now believe is what we recreational therapists do best. We use our interpersonal skills to assist our clients to achieve their potentials. We concentrate on positive experiences and fostering client strengths that allow our clients to exercise their actualizing tendencies. As clients become what they have the capability of becoming, they can remove or overcome barriers that prevent them from obtaining healthful lives.

In sum, providing diversional activities is one simple outcome that recreational therapists can offer. Another outcome of recreational therapy is the provision of recreational opportunities that negate negative emotions by producing positive emotions that lead clients to being open to expanding their horizons. Also important in recreational therapy is the provision of the treatments or interventions that reduce symptoms that occur with health problems. Most important, however, is that recreational therapists supply a positive, strengths-based perspective that can lead clients to overcome barriers to health and to enjoy the highest levels of health available to them.

Our Mission Includes Health Promotion

We recreational therapists assist our clients to deal with health problems by helping them to overcome or remove barriers to health. This primarily involves health protection as we intervene in our clients' lives by providing activities and recreational experiences that help clients to restore themselves following illnesses or disabilities that threaten their health.

Helping clients with poor health to restore their health has been the traditional role of recreational therapists. Health restoration was the original mission of recreational therapists who served in hospitals and other health care facilities during the formative years of the profession following World War II. Only clients faced with poor health received care from the early recreational therapists.

Happily, today clients do not have to be in poor health to receive recreational therapy services. Anyone wishing to improve his or her state of health may qualify to receive recreational therapy services. This is because recreational therapy services are delivered across the full spectrum of the illness/wellness continuum.

Let me explain the concept of the illness/wellness continuum. The illness/wellness continuum has poor health on one end (with the extreme being death) and high level health at the other (with optimal health or wellness being at the farthest point).

At the illness portion of the illness/wellness continuum, clients in poor health are suffering from conditions imposed by illnesses or disabilities. This state of poor health requires recreational therapists to assist them to deal with overcoming or removing barriers to health. Involved are interventions aimed at restoring the client's health, if at all possible, to what would be a normal state of health for him or her.

When dealing with extremely serious illness that may even be life threatening, it can be unrealistic to restore health back to normal for that individual. Here, maintaining a level of health or providing the highest quality of life possible for the person may be the goal. In most instances, however, recreational therapists work with clients to restore their health in the illness portion of the illness/wellness continuum.

Therefore, clients do not have to be "ill or disabled" to partake of recreational therapy services. Clients who are not ill or disabled can use recreational therapy to work toward health promotion or the achievement of an optimal level of health and wellness. This, I think, is positive, because including all who wish to improve their health as potential recreational therapy clients removes any stigma from having to be ill or disabled to take part in recreational therapy.

Clearly, the concept of health, under the concept of health promotion, is more than just the absence of illness. Those who seek optimal health hope to achieve high levels of mental and physical functioning. Virtually anyone who wishes to improve his or her state of health can be a candidate for health promotion programs.

Thus, today's recreational therapists do more than helping clients to restore health. Another important goal of recreational therapy has become health promotion. Our health promotion efforts allow clients to grow toward the highest levels of health and wellness possible for each of them as an individual.

In concluding this lesson, I should comment that for the sake of explanation I have talked about health restoration and health promotion as being entirely separate. In fact, many of our individual clients can profit from both health restoration and health promotion.

As recreational therapists, we often treat the client for health concerns while, at the same time, we begin to move toward health promotion programs that can have the effect of preventing the occurrence of the original health problem. For example, we may use interventions involving physical activity as a part of a treatment program to assist a client with bringing about stress reduction. Typically such treatment programs would be led or directed by the recreational therapist. This would be a program aimed at restoring health.

At the same time, we may begin to work with the client to educate him or her about the value of participating in physical activities. We also would be likely to give him or her the skills he or she needs to use physical exercise to achieve stress reduction once the client leaves our care. Here the client is assuming control with the help of the recreational therapist. This would be a program directed toward future health promotion as the client becomes empowered to use physical activities to combat stress in his or her everyday life.

Of course, the ultimate aim of recreational therapists is for clients to no longer need their services. As clients move along the illness/wellness continuum, they assume more and more control, and the role of the recreational therapist diminishes. Ideally, at the far end of the wellness part of the illness/wellness continuum, individuals assume responsibility for themselves and no longer require the services of a recreational therapist.

What Makes TR Therapeutic?

To me, being therapeutic implies an ability to produce a positive change in an individual's health. For example, bringing about desirable outcomes through the treatment of a disease or disorder would be therapeutic.

Simply providing recreation services to clients who are ill or disabled does not constitute the delivery of recreational therapy services, because there is no therapeutic intent involved. Without a planned intervention to bring about therapeutic benefit, what is being provided are simply recreation experiences, even though the services are being provided to persons who are ill or disabled.

In my mind, to be therapeutic, recreational therapy must display that it is purposeful and goal-directed in terms of supplying health benefits. The outcomes of recreational therapy are not random. They are planned. Recreational therapy employs an evidence-based approach that involves systematically using interventions to bring about specific therapeutic outcomes for clients.

How are therapeutic outcomes derived from recreational therapy? The answer is through the thorough application of the "recreational therapy process," sometimes referred to as the "therapeutic recreation process."

This recreational therapy process represents our systematic clinical approach to the achievement of therapeutic outcomes. It involves four phases: (a) assessment; (b) planning; (c) implementation; and (d) evaluation. Because the first letters of these four phases spell APIE, many speak of the therapeutic recreation process as the APIE (pronounced "A-pie") process.

Assessment is the first step in the recreational therapy process. It concerns collecting and analyzing data in order to determine the status of the client. Both client problems and strengths are assessed.

Next follows the planning phase. As a result of the assessment, the client's needs are identified. Needs are then prioritized, goals and objectives are formulated, strategies or actions to meet the goals are set, and methods are selected to assess progress toward the goals and objectives.

Implementation is the action phase. It involves the actual carrying out of the plan. At this stage, the recreational therapist provides the interventions that will allow clients to gain therapeutic benefits.

Evaluation is the final phase in the recreational therapy process. Here the question is answered: Were the plan and interventions effective in bringing about the sought outcomes?

The recreational therapy process is not at all restricted to hospitals, rehabilitation centers, mental health programs, or long-term care facilities. It can be applied anywhere when therapeutic outcomes are desired, even in community-based settings such as group homes or other organizations directed toward bringing about therapeutic benefits.

When questioning if the recreational therapy process was actually being followed in practice, my old friend and colleague, Jerry O'Morrow, used to joke that the APIE process was "A-pie in the sky." It is my view that a recreational therapist who does not follow the recreational therapy process should not claim to be doing recreational therapy. Without use of the systematic problem-solving process termed the recreational therapy process, no therapeutic intent can exist.

Do You Know Who We Are?

As much as I hate to admit it, I must confess that occasionally (okay, more than occasionally) I experience personal biases against occupational therapy. Yet I have to admit that one occupational therapy author has written something that I believe is profound. In his book, Conceptual Foundations of Occupational Therapy, Kielhofner (1997) wrote this about the importance of clear conceptual models for a profession:

> Members of a profession without a clear paradigm bear an undue burden in attempting to make sense of their life work. Perhaps the most pervasive impact of this paradigmatic uncertainly is the difficulty therapists have had with their own identity. Over the years, many students and colleagues have shared with me their frustrations in not being able to explain (to themselves, much less others) what their profession was. (p. 304)

I would expect that many in our profession would state something similar. I don't know how many times that I have heard students and young professionals complain that they were not able to explain just what our profession is about. This is a shame.

It is a shame on two levels. First, it is a shame that emerging professionals are frustrated by their inability to interpret their profession to others, or for themselves. Second, the leaders of our profession should feel shamed because of their lack of providing a clear definition of our profession. Let me talk about what I believe have been the reasons why this has occurred.

The major reason why emerging professionals cannot adequately explain their profession is not their fault. It is a direct result of the inadequate preparation they have been provided by their university professors. These professors have not exposed their students to conceptual models and how to analyze and evaluate them.

I have written elsewhere that: "Conceptual models of therapeutic recreation provide explicit frames of reference to describe…professional practice. They are means for us to articulate what is distinctive about our profession" (Austin, 1998, p. 109). Without an understanding of conceptual models for practice, as students and later as practitioners, those in our profession are almost certain to struggle to explain their profession.

Perhaps a reason for this is because the professors themselves do not really understand current conceptual models of practice and lack the knowledge and ability to analyze or evaluate practice models. My impression is that too many professors adopt one conceptual model that they "sell" to their students as the only model.

When students find the model they have been taught is lacking, they have little to fall back on. When young professionals find the model does not fit with their setting or area of practice, they have not been given alternative models to adopt or adapt. Therefore, students and young practitioners are naturally stymied in their attempts to interpret their profession.

Thus, I believe the major reason students and young practitioners cannot adequately explain their profession is because their professional preparation has been sadly lacking. I attribute this to university faculty who do not have the ability or inclination to really teach their students about the importance of conceptual models or the various models that have been developed. Further, I don't believe these educators have given their students the background to analyze and evaluate conceptual models. This puts emerging professionals in the position of not knowing how to examine conceptual models in order to decipher for themselves the foundations for their practice.

I might add that having seen this gap in professional preparation, I attempted to provide information for faculty and students to help in understanding conceptual models and how to analyze and evaluate them in a chapter published in 2002. For a discussion of conceptual models and how to analyze and evaluate them, you may wish to see my chapter titled "Conceptual Models in Therapeutic Recreation" in Austin, Dattilo, and McCormick's (2002) *Conceptual Foundations for Therapeutic Recreation*. It is my hunch, however, that even today university faculty are failing to provide students with the preparation they need to articulate to themselves or others what their profession is all about.

The second level on which we can lay the blame for the frustrations of emerging professionals to be able to describe our profession is more general. Health professions need to present definitional statements that interpret the profession to practitioners, students, kindred professions, insurance payers, legislative bodies, regulating agencies, and the public. The definitional statement should be relatively succinct, portraying the profession in a few sentences. I believe the profession as a whole has lacked the backbone to properly address the question as to who we are as a profession in a well-prepared definitional statement.

Let me explain. I have previously written about the necessity for any profession to define its boundaries. At that time, I "warned that without establishing clear boundaries therapeutic recreation would be doomed to basing professional preparation and practice on murky definitions that would not offer the clarity needed to advance the profession" (Austin, 2002, p. 2). Further, I wrote that the profession needed to clearly demarcate its boundaries "because carefully defining the profession will ultimately lead to the expansion of a focused and documented body of knowledge, provide students with a clear sense of mission and purpose, and differentiate therapeutic recreation from inclusive and special recreation" (p. 2).

My thoughts in making these statements had been strongly influenced by Dumas (1994) who had written:

> Boundaries enable us to set limits and to distinguish what to divide and separate. They denote the relative position of each entity within the organizational structure. Boundaries define roles, responsibilities, and prerogatives (of professions). (p. 13)

Without clear signals from our profession as to where our practice begins and ends (i.e., its boundaries) there is danger that it will be "all things to all people." And this is exactly where our profession is today—without clear boundaries and trying to be all things to all people.

Therefore, many see therapeutic recreation or recreational therapy as simply the provision of recreation services to persons who are ill and disabled. This is too bad.

The term "special recreation" has emerged to describe special recreation programs offered for persons who are ill or disabled. The Special Olympics is a prime example. The expression "inclusive recreation" has been developed to mean the provision of integrating those with disabilities into the recreation mainstream.

But neither the provision of special recreation or inclusive recreation should be included under either the expression "therapeutic recreation" or "recreational therapy." The use of either term, therapeutic recreation or recreational therapy, implies therapeutic intent. There is no therapeutic intent in special recreation or inclusive recreation, but there is clear intent of a planned therapeutic intervention in the terms therapeutic recreation and recreational therapy. After all, they explicitly use the expressions "therapeutic" and "therapy."

Unfortunately, national leaders have been slow to establish a definition of therapeutic recreation or recreational therapy that clearly demarcates the boundaries of our profession. In 2009, the American Therapeutic Recreation Association (ATRA) Board approved a new definition in an effort to better interpret the field to others. This action can be perceived as a good start toward gaining consensus on a definition. However, until there is a widespread consensus established, I believe there will remain confusion as to exactly what we do.

While on the topic, let me say that it is highly unfortunate that those in our profession have not settled on either the expression therapeutic recreation or recreational therapy to use as the one term referring to our profession. I believe that a case can be made for using either term, although the term recreational therapy would seem to be the best choice.

I personally favor adopting the term recreational therapy simply because the expression therapeutic recreation is so confusing to the general public. I have spoken to far too many United States senators and representatives and their staffers who have blank expressions when I use the term therapeutic recreation. They just don't "get it." When I say recreational therapy, these same individuals quickly understand. Even if they don't have a direct knowledge of the field, they will inquire if recreational therapy isn't something like physical therapy or occupational therapy, terms with which they are already acquainted.

I have encountered the same phenomenon when using the term "therapeutic recreation" in attempting to describe our profession to strangers in airports and to friends and family members not familiar with our profession. My guess is that you, if a student or member of our profession, have had similar experiences.

Beyond the confusion encountered when using the expression therapeutic recreation, I believe recreational therapy is a better term because it places the emphasis on therapy. We are first and foremost therapists. We are therapists who use prescriptive activities and recreation and leisure experiences to bring about therapeutic outcomes in our clients.

In contrast, the use of therapeutic recreation places the emphasis on recreation and the provision of recreation services. We are not simply recreators who happen to deliver recreation services to persons who are ill or disabled.

So I strongly believe that the term recreational therapy is much superior to the expression therapeutic recreation. The term recreational therapy is much better for interpreting our profession to others, and its emphasis on therapy clearly signals that our profession produces therapeutic outcomes.

I don't believe all the blame for the lack of a clear definition for our profession can be laid at the feet of university faculty who have failed to adequately explain conceptual models to students or at the feet of national leaders in our profession who have not been able to put the proper boundaries on their definitions of the profession. I suppose each of us has to assume some of the blame for our dilemma because we have not demanded that faculty or national leaders shoulder their responsibilities.

Nevertheless, I am personally frustrated by the clear lack of means for those of us in our profession to clearly portray our profession. I believe that to have an in-depth understanding of our profession, practitioners and students need to rely on knowledge of conceptual models that thoroughly describe the profession.

I further believe that our profession needs to adopt a concise definitional statement that establishes the boundaries of our profession.

I have arrived at my own definition of our profession. It follows:

Recreational therapy uses a systematic four-step process involving assessment, planning, implementation, and evaluation to bring about therapeutic outcomes with clients who wish to improve their levels of health through participation in activities that have the potential to produce recreational or leisure experiences.

Perhaps my definition will be of use to those who attempt to interpret their profession to others. I hope so. By the way, my definition flows out of the conceptual model that I developed. The model has appeared widely in the literature (e.g., Austin, 2009) and is termed the Health Protection/Health Promotion Model.

In ending this lesson, let me conclude by stating: (a) there exists a real lack of a clear and unified message for those in our profession to answer the question: "What does your profession do?", and (b) educators in their classrooms and professionals in national leadership roles need to address this question so that no one needs to put his or her head down in shame because he or she has not been properly prepared to answer this basic question of who we are as a profession. Am I correct?

Recreational Therapists Need a Philosophy of Practice

I first got to know good friend of mine Jerry Kelley when he was on faculty at the University of Illinois at the time I was at the university working on my Ph.D. Jerry had a rich practitioner background that included working as a recreational therapist at the Illinois State Psychiatric Institute and as a colleague of the famous American psychiatrist Karl Menninger. Menninger was one of the founders of the Menninger Clinic and a highly influential author and member of the medical profession in the decades of the 1950s and 1960s. And, by the way, Menninger was also a strong advocate for recreational therapy.

Jerry held that it was critical that recreational therapists form a solid philosophy of practice. I can recall discussing this with him in what turned out to be a lengthy and heated debate. It was my position then that it was what the recreational therapist did with the client that was vital, and that as long as there were positive outcomes from this interaction, that a philosophy of practice did not matter. Further, I argued, practitioners have busy lives. They don't have time to "philosophize." Philosophy in my mind was something abstract, something for academics to ponder. Boy, was I wrong!

Jerry argued persuasively that a philosophy of practice provided a set of values and beliefs that formed a basic foundation to guide practice. The recreational therapist's philosophy, he said, determined his or her roles and relationships, as well the policies and procedures of practice that he or she followed. He said, in fact, that how a practitioner acts on a day-to-day basis is strongly influenced by that person's philosophy of practice because it helps the practitioner to solve dilemmas, set priorities, and to guide decisions that have to be made each day. Further, Jerry stated that without a well-formed philosophy of practice that a therapist cannot be a reflective practitioner who examines what he or she does and why. Finally, he commented that probably every recreational therapist actually held a philosophy of practice even if he or she had not thought deeply about it, nor had explicitly stated it.

Once I heard Jerry's arguments, although at first it was hard for me to admit, I had to concede to him that he was right. I did in fact hold values and beliefs that served to guide my practice, even if I had not given extensive thought to exactly what these were. The more I thought about it, the more I had to agree with Jerry that a philosophy of practice was important, perhaps critical, because it affected almost everything I would do as a practitioner.

As a professor, I eventually became to believe that it was so important to form a philosophy of practice that all of the recreational therapy students I instructed in their university studies were made to examine their personal philosophies of practice. This, I felt, would provide them with a basis for what they would do when they became recreational therapists.

Somewhere I recall reading that Socrates stated that the unexamined life was not worth living. Perhaps this can be restated in the terms that an unexamined professional practice by a recreational therapist is not worth doing. It is critical that recreational therapists are reflective practitioners who examine what they are doing and why they are doing it. This keeps us from doing things simply because "that's the way we've always done it," which is a trap the unthinking recreational therapist can fall into. The best recreational therapists are thoughtful, not habitual, in their practice.

Thus, today I would strongly advise all recreational therapists to examine their own philosophies of practice. This starts with examining professional values.

The beliefs to which we most strongly cling to constitute our value systems. These help to shape our behaviors. So it is necessary that all helping professionals, including recreational therapists, become aware of their values.

From a list of professional values I prepared for my most recent textbook (Austin, 2009, p. 244), examples of professional values include the following: (a) valuing their role in assisting people to achieve optimal levels of health; (b) viewing clients as needing autonomy so they may maintain as much control as possible over their lives. (c) seeing the client-therapist relationship as a key element in recreational therapy; (d) valuing a strength-based approach to health enhancement that perceives each client as someone possessing abilities and intact strengths that can be used to meet challenges; (e) valuing fun and enjoyment as motivators for clients; (f) seeing the client, not the activity, as their focus; (g) valuing therapeutic recreation for being purposeful and goal-directed; (h) valuing every client as an individual possessing intrinsic worth who should be treated with dignity; and (i) assuming it is their obligation to offer competent and ethical care to their clients.

I present these values as illustrations. Each individual holds strong to his or her own values developed as he or she has gone through life. It is this personalized set of values of that each recreational therapist needs to become aware.

Basic philosophical beliefs about human nature may be seen to constitute a second major element in each individual's philosophy of practice. It is therefore necessary that we recreational therapists look closely at our basic philosophical beliefs in order to develop understandings of our total philosophies of practice.

Here again from my recent textbook (Austin, 2009, pp. 245-246) come some examples of possible philosophical beliefs that draw on an original list presented by Brill and Levine (2002). These include philosophical beliefs such as holding that: (a) human beings are social animals who need to interact with other individuals; (b) people exist in relationship with others with this relationship being one in which mutual rights and responsibilities are given and received; (c) both the welfare of the individual and the welfare of the group must be considered; (d) humans and all living things possess intrinsic worth: (e) all people possess a need to grow toward realizing their unique potentials; (f) both the individual and society can be understood; and (g) all individuals have the capacity for change.

A basis for a philosophy of practice comes out of recreational therapists gaining a grasp of the beliefs that make up their value systems and identifying their basic philosophical beliefs about human nature. When identifying professional values and philosophical beliefs about human nature the recreational therapist should also assess just how strongly he or she holds each of his or her values and beliefs. There are sure to be some values and beliefs to which each of us are most committed and will therefore have the greatest impact on practice. Acknowledging which values and beliefs are most important is a means to refine our philosophies of practice.

Because I firmly believe that each of us holds a philosophy of practice that influences what we do every day as a recreational therapist, I do not believe that we should stop with completing only an initial analysis of our philosophies of practice. I would suggest that because we are evolving as individuals each of us needs to constantly examine our philosophy of practice so that we understand it and can react to it as a reflective practitioner.

It should be mentioned that mature professions have a set of common beliefs that are held by those in the profession. Holding similar beliefs unifies the profession's practice. Without such a set of common beliefs, there will exist no shared philosophy of practice and therefore little consensus about how to practice. I believe the recreational therapy profession is still in the process of developing such a unified philosophy of practice.

I would hope that understandings from this lesson will encourage recreational therapists to acknowledge the vital need for recreational therapy practice to be based on well-developed philosophies of practice. Further, I would hope that each individual recreational therapist would examine his or her own philosophy of practice and then work with others in the profession to identify commonalities so that the profession can ultimately develop a unified philosophy of practice.

In closing, I would like to thank Jerry Kelley for helping me to understand that there exists an integral relationship between philosophy and practice. I suppose at some point in time that I would have eventually come to understand the critical nature of a philosophy of practice. But Jerry sharing his insights with me was certainly influential in molding my thinking.

The Importance of Recreation and Leisure

What goes through your mind when you hear the words recreation and leisure? Unfortunately, for many individuals, the terms recreation and leisure conjure up images of frivolous fun.

This is too bad, because recreation and leisure are just the opposite of frivolous. Instead of lacking importance, they represent serious concepts that can have tremendous impacts on human beings and should not be taken lightly. They are consequential and substantial forces that should hold high places in our culture.

In my writings, I have professed that a vital characteristic of recreational therapists is a strong belief in the power of recreation and leisure. I have stated, "Recreational therapists prize the positive consequences to be gained through meaningful recreation and leisure experiences" (Austin, 2009, p. 237).

Recreation and leisure have been seen to be important since the early history of humans. No less than the great Greek philosopher Aristotle stressed the importance of recreation and leisure (Iso-Ahola, 1980).

I must admit that I have not deeply studied the literature interpreting the scholarly conceptualizations of leisure first introduced by Aristotle. Perhaps it is just as well that I haven't taken up too much time of my time in reading about leisure if Simpson and Yoshioka (1992) are correct in stating that "Aristotelian conceptions of leisure are poorly understood and misinterpreted" in the writings of most leisure scholars!

I have examined Aristotelian concepts of leisure enough to know that leisure held an extremely lofty place in his philosophy. It was Aristotle's view that work is something people do in order to attain leisure, and that leisure is the way to happiness and quality of life because it provides a means to self-fulfillment through intellectual, physical, and spiritual growth (Hemingway, 1996; Iso-Ahola, 1980; Simpson & Yoshioka, 1992).

Thus, to Aristotle and the Greeks, leisure was anything but idle time. It represented a major life activity that had as its purpose self-realization or the cultivation of the self to the fullest. The Aristotelian vision of leisure was that it was as a means to achieving excellence as a human being and, as Hemingway (1988) has written, "human excellence lies in the highest achievement of human function," according to Aristotle.

Recreation does not seem to hold as high a place as leisure in the order of things according to Aristotle. Yet recreation was seen as important because it provided rest and refreshment. Recreation was seen by Aristotle as having a healing function. Through recreation people restored their minds and bodies (Grube, 1995).

Thus, Aristotle saw recreation as a way to "re-create" or rejuvenate oneself in order to bring oneself back to what was normal for the individual. The focus of leisure, on the other hand, was the "virtuous action" (Hemingway, 1996) of the achievement of self-fulfillment.

While scholarly discourse on recreation and leisure has not been a staple in the recreational therapy literature, some attention has been given to the Aristotelian view. Two authors in particular have used an Aristotelian perspective as a foundation for therapeutic recreation practice. Widmer and Ellis (1998) have suggested that there is a close connection between leisure and quality of life that needs be recognized by recreational therapists.

Perhaps the conceptual model for our profession that most closely subscribes to the Aristotelian view of recreation and leisure is my own Health Protection/Health Promotion Model. If you are familiar with my model, you will recall that recreation is seen as activities that are restorative. I have written that "Through recreation, clients may regain their equilibrium so they may once again resume their quest for actualization" (Austin, 2009, p. 175). Under my model, leisure is seen to be intrinsically motivated, self-determined behavior that permits clients to stretch themselves through growth-producing activities so they may achieve high-level wellness. Those who enjoy high-level wellness, in turn, have freedom from barriers to health and are therefore able to pursue self-actualization (Austin, 2009).

Thus, recreation and leisure are concepts that must be taken seriously by recreational therapists. In fact, recreation and leisure are the cornerstones of recreational therapy.

Recreational Therapists Use a Strength-Based Approach

People generally prefer to take part in recreational activities in which they perform very well. If they are good swimmers, they like to swim. If they are strong bikers, they enjoy biking. If they excel at tennis, they want to play tennis, and so on.

The lone exception to this rule seems to be golf. I would say that most golfers are not really all that proficient at the sport. In fact, many who play regularly are high handicappers. Yet, golfers by the millions keep going out to hit a little white ball and follow it around the golf course for some reason. But golf is a real exception to the rule that we typically like to participate in those recreational activities in which we excel.

The fact that people like activities in which they do well is probably why almost all recreational therapists when doing the initial assessment interview ask their new clients what activities they enjoy. This is an indirect way of finding out what activities clients do well.

Knowing the activities that clients do well provides recreational therapists with valuable data. This information provides insights into some of the strengths of clients.

We recreational therapists can then help our clients through an optimistic, positive approach that uses their strengths to "take the high side" in overcoming barriers that threaten health. This approach of the recreational therapist is simply using each client's strengths to place the emphasis on what is right with the client rather than on what is wrong. The focus is on the positive, not the client's pathology.

One of the most insightful works that I have encountered is a book by Glicken (2004) titled *Using the Strengths Perspective in Social Work Practice: A Positive Approach for the Helping Professional.* While written by a professor of social work, it seems to me that its contents reflect the beliefs I hold and those held by many recreational therapists.

According to Glicken, our colleagues in mental health often mistakenly take a pessimistic view of the clients we serve. His claim is that many times self-help groups are better at bringing about changes in mental health than are professionals because these groups are supportive and provide a strengths perspective that focuses on what is right with individuals.

I tend to agree with Glicken that most people have a lot more about them that is positive and functional than negative or dysfunctional. This healthy part of the person contains many strengths that can become the focus for recreational therapy.

My observations of successful case after successful case in recreational therapy tell me that Glicken is correct when he says clients typically show more improvement when the focus is on what is right about them instead of their pathology.

One of the earliest successes that used a strengths approach occurred with one of the patients that I came to know in my first professional position as a recreational therapist at a psychiatric hospital. The patient was an African-American man with a good physique who was in his early 30s. He was admitted to the hospital after encountering severe depression.

It turned out that this patient had been a track man in college and, as I recall, he had enjoyed great success with his track career. But he had not run or worked out regularly following his graduation from college. At the urging of one of the recreational therapists, he began to run again at the hospital. I can recall seeing him dashing around the campus on the daily run that he took early every morning.

In the early 1960s, running had not yet gained popularity, so runners didn't have the high-tech running shoes we commonly see today. The patient, as I recall, wore a pair of high-top black basketball shoes while running in shorts and a T-shirt. Yet, even without all the gear we have today, he was quite a striking figure as he ran on the roads that crisscrossed the hospital's campus.

Because running was an oddity on the campus of our hospital, the patient quickly became known as the guy who ran every morning. People waived to him as he took his morning run. Others commented to him that they had seen him running and admired his effort of running on a daily basis. As time went on, staff would sometimes be seen accompanying the patient on one of his runs.

It was only a matter of weeks until this young man was able to overcome his depression and be released from the hospital. I am sure that this patient received drug therapy for his depression. Yet, I think that using the almost forgotten skill of running played a large role his recovery.

I believe that getting out every day for a run activated and motivated this young man. Further, he was able to reactivate the positive feelings that he enjoyed as a track man during his college days. These positive feelings only got stronger and stronger as his running helped return him to a fitness level that he had not experienced in years. Finally, in addition to the intrinsic motivation he gained from his running, he gained a great deal of positive feedback from staff and other patients who complimented him on his running. I think these positive comments were bound to have enhanced his self-esteem.

In short, by using a strength he possessed, I believe this young man was able to overcome the problem that brought him into the hospital and to regain interest in an activity in which he excelled. I think his case provides an excellent illustration of how the strength-based approach works.

I should mention that strengths other than abilities in recreational activities can be used by recreational therapy clients. Personality traits such as persistence, determination, resilience, or creativity may be strengths that clients may use. Other strengths might include skills such as coping skills, interpersonal skills, or communication skills. Still other strengths could be past successes they have had in their lives, including educational successes.

In this lesson, I have restricted my discussion to strengths related to recreational participation that can be used by clients to overcome problems and to enhance their levels of health and well-being. In another lesson, I will give attention to how clients can use other types of strengths to protect and promote their levels of health.

Client Strengths Include Traits and Resources

We in recreational therapy often first think of recreational abilities when we consider client strengths. This is natural since we regularly draw upon our clients' recreational talents.

In addition to recreational strengths, people possess strengths in the form of personality traits and resources to which they have access. Desirable personality traits that become client strengths include hope, optimism, bravery, perseverance, determination, resilience, social intelligence, personal intelligence, emotional intelligence, forgiveness, self-control, kindness, gratitude, and humor, to name a few (Glicken, 2004).

Resources that can be strengths for clients include supportive elements in their lives, including family, friends, colleagues, and their community. These are resources that clients can turn to for support in times of crisis.

The recreational therapist needs to build a list of potential client strengths when collecting assessment data on the client. Strengths assessment should include positive personality traits and resources the client can draw upon, as well as recreational abilities. This information then forms the client's strengths list.

It should be mentioned that clients may possess untapped strengths that they may not even be aware they have. The assessment process can be a time of self-discovery as clients begin to realize their own strengths.

Recreational therapists tend to emphasize the positive. Thus, the high level of attention given to the assessment of client strengths is very much a part of the tradition of recreational therapy of focusing on clients' positive traits and abilities.

In completing the assessment of a client's strengths, it is likely that it will be helpful to examine those aspects in the client's life that have been positive. Strengths can be transferred from one part of life to another so identifying strengths revealed in looking at the positive parts of the client's life can be helpful in assisting the client to realize these strengths can often serve him or her well in overcoming problematic parts in his or her life.

For example, a client may have regularly displayed strengths, such as persistence, integrity, nurturance, and humor while being successful at work. These same traits may be applied in another area of life, such as maintaining social relationships, in which the client is encountering difficulties.

It is also important that assessment uncover areas of potential strengths for clients. Clients often possess traits or even potential resources they have not tapped. Recreational therapists can work with clients to develop these potential areas of strength once these have been identified. Previously unrealized and undeveloped strengths can become cultivated so they become tools for clients to use to overcome problems or achieve their potentials.

An example of a trait that a client might not have recognized and developed would be creativity. Given the opportunity to participate in creative arts, a client could discover an affinity for expressive writing or poetry. Another client might discover that his sense of humor can become a means to stress reduction by using it to provide a break from stressors.

Still another example might be a client discovering a community resource that could offer services that would be highly supportive of the client. A community Y, for instance, might offer yoga classes that would be helpful to a client in achieving relaxation.

What is key is that traits and resources join recreational abilities for those employing a strengths perspective in recreational therapy. Once identified and developed, client strengths offer a foundation for change.

Recreational Therapy is Action Oriented, but the Emphasis is on the Client and Not on the Activity

We in recreational therapy are action oriented, rather than talk oriented. When people think of recreational therapy, they typically think of clients actively participating in activities of some type. Because activities have such an apparent place within recreational therapy, those who are uninitiated may see activities as being the prominent feature of the profession.

But, as one of my favorite sports analysts, Lee Corso would say, "Not so fast, my friend!" While activities play an important part in recreational therapy, they are only a means and not an end.

The end is what happens to the client as a result of participation in an activity. Thus, we hold to the basic tenet that the emphasis in recreational therapy is always on the client and not on the activity itself.

I can recall that as a young recreational therapist, I suffered from a major weakness in my approach to leading activities. My weakness had to do with being too absorbed with the activity itself instead of the effect it might have on my clients.

For example, I worried about the rules and procedures for games when leading them, rather on concentrating on what was happening with my clients as a result of their participation. This was because I was not familiar with the games and therefore was not comfortable with my ability to lead them. Therefore, my focus was self-centered and not client-centered as it should have been.

I eventually learned that in order to help clients gain full therapeutic benefit from any activity, I had to be thoroughly conversant with the activity so it was second nature to me. This allowed me to focus my attention fully on what was happening to my clients in terms of gaining therapeutic outcomes from their participation, which was why I was conducting the activity to begin with.

So instead of being "featured characters," activities are only the "supporting characters" in recreational therapy. Recreational therapy activities are means by which clients gain therapeutic outcomes such as experiencing positive emotions, building skills they can use in their everyday lives, enhancing their self-views, or having experiences through which they can learn about themselves and how they interact with others.

In short, activities are not the focus of recreational therapy. Instead, activities are simply vehicles through which therapeutic outcomes are realized.

Recreation and Leisure Activities Provide Fun with a Purpose

In their book titled *Healthy Pleasures*, Ornstein and Sobel (1989) state that "the healthiest people seem to be pleasure-loving, pleasure-seeking, pleasure-creating individuals" (p.7). These authors proclaim that those who enjoy the highest levels of health are not self-absorbed health fanatics but those who are engaged in healthy pleasures. They go on to suggest that healthy individuals do not deny themselves pleasures but instead take full advantage of their leisure to participate in satisfying, enriching activities that bring about positive feelings and mood enhancement. In short, the authors of *Healthy Pleasures* strongly believe in the premise that the things we enjoy (i.e., our pleasures) are likely to be good for us and make us healthier.

In a way, recreational therapy can be thought to be the systemization of healthy pleasures. Recreational therapy systematically employs enjoyable activities to bring about beneficial outcomes.

To paraphrase a popular song, for recreational therapy clients activities are "the honey that makes the medicine taste good." Enjoyable activities are the means by which people restore or improve their health in recreational therapy.

I believe that fun, enjoyment, and pleasure are unique, positive components of our profession of recreational therapy that we employ every day to improve the health and well-being of our clients. The value of recreational therapy is perhaps most evident in hospitals, long-term care facilities, and other clinical settings where patients or clients are faced with cold, sterile surroundings. The elements of fun, enjoyment, and pleasure are relatively unique within such clinical environments and may likely only be found when recreational therapists are available to help clients to take part in activities that allow the fun, enjoyment, and pleasure typically missing from their lives.

But recreational therapy goes beyond the simple provision of fun, enjoyment, and pleasure. Although having fun, enjoyment, and pleasure are certainly good, they are not the ultimate ends in themselves but, instead, are means to the end of a healthier life.

People exercise their strengths and abilities in successfully taking part in recreational or leisure activities. Typically individuals further develop and refine their strengths and abilities through their continuing participation in those self-reinforcing activities defined as recreation or leisure. From recreation and leisure participation positive feelings result (e.g., fun, enjoyment, pleasure, satisfaction, confidence).

Two favorable occurrences result from recreation and leisure experiences. One is the development of positive strengths or abilities. Building strengths and abilities provides means for individuals to move toward overcoming distress and to grow toward high level health and well-being.

The other occurrence resulting from recreation and leisure experiences is the production of positive emotions. Such positive feelings offer impetus for change as people become more optimistic and more apt to risk new behaviors or new ways of thinking that can lead to change.

I can recall my boss, Al Grubb, at Evansville State Hospital in Indiana, talking about how recreation activities were the recreational therapist's "tools for treatment." By this, he meant that the psychiatric patients we treated were able to use recreational activities to experience positive feelings (e.g., fun, enjoyment, pleasure, success, satisfaction) and to build their strengths.

Resulting positive emotions helped our patients to combat negative emotions and to feel better about themselves so that they might have more optimistic viewpoints and the confidence in themselves they needed to face their problems in mental health and to overcome them. The strengths (e.g., social skills, enhanced self-esteem, problem-solving abilities, recreational skills, and personality traits such as perseverance) they built through their participation in activities provided them with the resources they needed to be successful in their interactions with others.

Thus, recreation and leisure activities offer more for individuals than just fun, enjoyment, and pleasure. The value of recreation and leisure activities exceeds these immediate outcomes by offering participants purposeful means to build the personal resources they need to enjoy healthy lives. The activities of recreational therapy then truly do represent fun with a purpose.

The Therapeutic Relationship is at the Heart of Recreational Therapy

I think one of the first things I became aware of as a young recreational therapist was just how important it was to establish good therapist/client relationships. If I had the trust of a client and I liked that client and the client liked me, we had a relationship that really seemed to be a foundation for a therapeutic alliance.

Today more than ever, I believe that therapeutic relationships are at the core of all interventions regardless of clients' specific concerns. They are the medium through which we help our clients to overcome obstacles to health and to grow toward the highest levels of wellness possible for them.

The trust factor in therapeutic relationships is a key element. If clients trust us, they will openly share their thoughts and feelings with us and know we will keep their confidences. They will see us as believing in them and their capacities for change. They will understand that we don't want to control them, and that we wish for them to act as independently as possible. They will sense that we are there to support them and to provide the assistance they need. They will believe that we care about them and that we want to act in their best interests.

My personal belief is that recreational therapists enjoy wonderful positions from which to build therapeutic relationships with clients. For one thing, recreational therapists are generally seen by clients to be warm, good-natured individuals whose role it is to do things with clients that they like. This gets us off to a good start with clients.

In our roles as recreational therapists, we are not seen as persons who have great power or control over clients, as a medical doctor would. We are on more of an equal footing with our clients. Also, unlike doctors, we don't do things to clients, like giving medical examinations. As I am fond of saying, recreational therapists do things *with* clients, not *to* clients.

My next point about the abilities of recreational therapists to establish therapeutic relationships follows closely from the prior point of not being seen as individuals in controlling roles. That is, that as a basic principle of their practice, recreational therapists constantly strive to permit their clients to assume as much choice and control as they can. This attitude of giving control to clients often stands out in the controlling atmospheres that too frequently are found in clinical settings.

But perhaps the greatest advantage that recreational therapists have in establishing therapeutic relationships is the amount of quality time they spend with clients. Unlike the doctor who may have to dash in and out of client appointments or the social worker who has only a few minutes to spend with clients, recreational therapists tend to spend a great amount of time interacting with their clients.

Typically therapist/client interactions in recreational therapy take part during regularly scheduled programs. These are instances when clients are likely to experience fun and enjoyment and share common experiences with their recreational therapists. Often the activities are ones in which clients and recreational therapists work together toward achieving some positive outcome (e.g., completing a craft project or learning a new recreational skill) and such joint participation helps form bonds. Even early on in recreational therapy groups, icebreaking activities help build rapport as therapists and clients get to know one another.

Also, by spending time with clients, recreational therapists can take time to talk with clients. Not only can they talk, but more importantly, they can listen to clients as well. Through listening, recreational therapists can develop and display empathetic understandings of the clients' perspectives. Regular chances for interactions with clients additionally provide recreational therapists opportunities to indicate positive regard for clients by displaying authentic warmth and nonjudgmental attitudes towards them. Most agree that developing empathetic understandings and expressing positive regard for clients are basic to building therapeutic relationships.

You may recall from reading Carl Rogers' (1961) thoughts in other lessons of this book that another basic component in therapeutic relationships, in his view, is being genuine with clients. I think the amount of time recreational therapists spend with clients helps them to establish that they are being honest and sincere with clients. All of us know that sustained relationships are ones where people are honest and open with one another and where false promises are not made. Recreational therapists have the time needed with clients to display to them that they are being genuine.

Finally, recreational therapy activities typically are ones where recreational therapists establish environments that are safe and enjoyable and where clients are not judged and are treated with respect. Within such a setting, clients can feel comfortable to relax, "let their hair down," and be themselves, because they sense the atmosphere is a nonjudgmental one where they will be treated respectfully.

Therapeutic relationships are indeed basic foundations from which to help clients to obtain therapeutic benefits. We, as recreational therapists, are very lucky to hold the positive roles that we do with clients and to be able to demonstrate the principles and values of our profession that assist us to enjoy therapeutic relationships with our clients.

Recreational Therapy Offers a Unique, Caring Atmosphere

I hold as a core belief that the provision of the warm, supportive, caring environment typically represented within recreational therapy is a virtue that few therapies can claim. Within this unique, beneficial atmosphere, clients are provided a safe and accepting place to deal with their concerns and to grow toward meeting their potentials.

The basis for the caring atmosphere found in recreational therapy is an approach represented within the history of recreational therapy. Recreational therapy had its beginnings with the provision of a caring atmosphere within large, impersonal institutions. Being rooted in that history, caring has always played a discernible role in recreational therapy.

The caring philosophy of recreational therapy is built on a belief in human dignity and preserving the dignity of those being cared for. Recreational therapists respect their clients and value them as persons of worth.

The caring attitude displayed by recreational therapists is clearly reflected in their behaviors as they strive to connect with clients through the provision of empathetic responses. Recreational therapists want to learn from their clients what their clients are going through and to relate the understandings they develop back to their clients.

Further, recreational therapists avoid being critical of clients or being directive with clients. Recreational therapists are facilitative, not manipulative or controlling. They believe clients possess abilities to take responsibility for themselves and therefore support their clients in their efforts to assume personal responsibility for change. In short, recreational therapists continually attempt to maximize freedom, autonomy, and choice making on the part of their clients.

The warm, supportive, caring atmosphere also frees clients to be themselves. It is a safe environment, one unencumbered by restrictions, where clients can freely express themselves and experience joy and pleasure through their play and recreation. This opens clients up to explore their potentials and to discover their strengths and abilities.

Caring in recreational therapy is never taking advantage of the vulnerability of clients with illnesses or disabilities. Instead, recreational therapists become interconnected with their clients by entering into a partnership through which they work toward improving the health of each of their clients.

Thus, recreational therapists prize the client/therapist relationship. They reach out to clients in contrast to those who don't really care about clients and close themselves off from their clients. Those who don't extend themselves to clients lack the human connectedness that is a real part of recreational therapy.

Offering visible support through establishing a warm, supportive, caring atmosphere to me displays the compassion that recreational therapists have for their clients. It is an atmosphere that can be a powerful tool in client care.

Recreational Therapy is Customized Care

It is tempting for emerging recreational therapists to think that there should be a treatment approach that works for each medical or psychiatric diagnosis or for each type of disability. Under such a model, once the client's condition was known, the recreational therapist could then simply apply the indicated protocol that would provide therapeutic benefit for that condition.

It might be thought to be nice if such a mechanistic approach could be successful in recreational therapy. Such an approach is destined to failure, however, when applied to complex human beings who have the right to exercise self-determination in their own care. In this chapter, I will explain why this approach, which at first blush seems to make common sense, is faulty and why a customized care approach is superior.

Recreational therapy never follows the "one-size-fits-all" approach initially outlined above. Instead, recreational therapy reflects customized care for clients. Customized care focuses on individualized care planning to meet client needs while considering client strengths and client preferences.

A major reason why recreational therapists follow a customized care model rather than a "one-size-fits-all" model is that clients have very different needs. Each client is assessed by the recreational therapist to determine exactly what needs he or she may have that recreational therapy can help meet. Even clients with an identical medical diagnosis may have very different needs that can be addressed within recreational therapy.

Another reason for customized care is that recreational therapy is a profession in which practitioners really do care about their clients as individuals. Valuing clients as individuals sets up a scenario that leads to each client being treated in a special way. Because clients are individuals who are not alike, they not only have different needs but they have unique strengths and varying preferences that recreational therapists take into consideration.

Many of the differences clients possess are in terms of the strengths they bring to the helping situation. A client may have highly developed recreational abilities. Another client may possess personality traits such as optimism, perseverance, courage, or creativity. Still another client may have a strong social support system in the form of friends or family that are willing to provide assistance. It is up to the recreational therapist to help the client to identify strengths that may prove to be useful in planning a care program.

Individual clients also have preferences that need to be honored. Recreational therapists value involving clients in the design of their care to the greatest extent possible. Client independence and choice are seen as being key elements in recreational therapy. Each recreational therapist wishes to join with each individual client in a partnership that allows the client to proceed on a path to recovery or growth that appeals to him or her. Thus recreational therapists support clients in making self-directed decisions regarding their care.

For example, a means to client self-determination would be for the recreational therapist to review the nature of possible recreational therapy groups with a client so he or she might select the group that has the best fit for his or her needs and strengths. Such an approach offers an informed, client-centered decision-making process that assures the client's preferences are honored.

Of course, there are times when clients are not ready to make completely self-determined decisions about their care. Due to diminished mental capacity or the possibility of a decision leading to a dangerous situation for the client or others, instances may occur when some amount of coercion may be needed for the client's own good. Nevertheless, as a general rule, recreational therapists prize maximizing clients' decision making and involvement in the selection of their care plans.

In sum, an individualized client-centered approach involving client self-determination helps assure that plans are customized to fit the exact needs of each client. A therapist-directed, "one-size-fits-all" approach to care in which client involvement is minimized is not valued within recreational therapy.

Recreational Therapy as a Dress Rehearsal for Life

It takes practice in order to refine new skills or new behaviors. Recreational therapy offers a safe, supportive environment in which to learn and to try out new skills and new behaviors.

Some skills may be both learned and practiced in recreational therapy programs. Social skills training comes to mind as an example of a set of skills that may be taught in a structured recreational therapy program. Then, as social skills are learned, they may be tried out in social recreation programs (e.g., dances) provided by recreational therapy.

In other instances, skills or behaviors may be learned outside of recreational therapy, but recreational therapy programs may offer opportunities for clients to try out and to practice what they have learned. For example, clients may learn new ways of behaving in a counseling group but not be able to work on their new behaviors within the time allotted for their counseling group. In this example, clients may use their participation in almost any recreational therapy group to perfect their new behaviors. Another approach is for the recreational therapy staff to be briefed by the counseling staff on what behaviors are being worked on in the counseling group. Recreational therapy sessions can then be specifically structured to allow for those behaviors to be practiced, and staff can be alerted to reinforce clients for positive demonstrations of those behaviors.

Recreational therapy can also offer clients opportunities for rehearsals or role-playing for future situations. An instance might be practicing social situations that are difficult for clients. Recreational therapy can offer a safe, even playful, atmosphere in which clients can experiment with behaviors they are learning.

Still other instances of recreational therapists supplying opportunities for rehearsals are community reintegration programs. Within these programs recreational therapists accompany clients on community outings, so that skills such as riding a bus, using a wheelchair to negotiate urban environments, or ordering a meal in a restaurant may be rehearsed prior to returning from a rehabilitation center to full community living. Such community reintegration programs are common for clients undergoing cognitive rehabilitation, physical rehabilitation, and psychiatric rehabilitation.

In any case, it is crucial that clients are able to transfer their skills and behaviors from a learning environment to an environment where skills may be practiced. Recreational therapists regularly offer clients opportunities to make that transfer. Of course, the ultimate transfer is when clients transfer their learning from clinical settings to their real life settings.

The WHO Definition of Health and Its Acceptance by Recreational Therapists

The traditional biomedical model of health has dealt strictly with the absence of disease. This view of health is set in the context of avoiding deviations from accepted biological norms.

A much wider multidimensional view of health came with the World Health Organization (WHO) definition of health that included physical, mental, and social well-being. The complete WHO definition read that health was "a state of complete physical, mental, and social well being and not merely the absence of disease or infirmity" (World Health Organization, 1948).

The expression "biopsychosocial health" was adopted to encompass WHO's new way of thinking about health, because it included biological, psychological, and social aspects of health. We also began to hear the term "quality of life" employed to capture the notion that health extended far beyond the absence of illness.

The profession of recreational therapy was still in its infancy in the mid-twentieth century during the inception of WHO's extended conceptualization of health. As a result, recreational therapy was a profession that was exposed early in its development to WHO's expanded concept of health.

Most in our emerging profession seemed to quickly adopt the WHO view of health that included each person's physical, mental, and social well-being. Recreational therapists generally came to recognize the interrelated influences of biological aspects, psychological dynamics, and social relationships, including family and community support systems on health.

By the time I began my career in the early 1960s, WHO's expanded view of health had become widely accepted within our profession. Recreational therapists tended to understand the effect illnesses have on the total functioning of clients (physically, psychologically, and socially), and that their approach necessarily had to be holistic.

This holistic approach to health by recreational therapists of course was rooted in the belief that health rests on psychological and social as well as biological factors. Such a belief produced direct ramifications for practice. Because the total person is a concern of recreational therapy, the whole person becomes the focus of clinical interventions. In short, the province of recreational therapy is seen as the functioning of the entire person.

To some degree recreational therapy may have become handicapped because it has generally subscribed to WHO's extended model of health. This is because many in the medical community have remained allied to the old biomedical model and therefore have been slow to appreciate recreational therapy's holistic approach to health.

Under the old biomedical model, the disease is diagnosed, and then a treatment is selected to cure it without concern for the whole person or the impact of the illness on the individual's everyday functional capacity. Nor do those following the biological disease model tend to focus on how individuals may be prepared and strengthened so they develop the functional capacity to better meet future obstacles to health. With this narrow view of health and disease dominating their work, you can appreciate why these health providers may not fully embrace recreational therapists' much broader approach to client care.

Further, recreational therapy does not define the total person solely by their disease, as those who practice traditional medicine have. Recreational therapists realize that individuals differ a great deal in terms of their symptomatology, living situations, self-views, strengths, and resources. Recreational therapists also recognize that diseases and their treatments may impact various aspects of the total person. For example, physical disorders and their treatment may produce psychological effects and psychological disorders may lead to difficulties in social relationships.

Because of their approach, I see recreational therapists taking a large role in the care of those children and adults who must deal with chronic illnesses. These are individuals for whom there is not a medical cure for their disorders.

I would anticipate that recreational therapists will play a particularly crucial role in the future in serving the growing number of older Americans with chronic health problems. These persons will not be able to cast aside their chronic illnesses. Yet they will want to live their lives to the fullest extent possible. For persons with chronic illnesses, the holistic clinical approach of recreational therapy would seem to be an ideal match to help them to achieve optimal functioning in their daily lives.

Let me sum up by stating that recreational therapy shares with traditional medicine oriented health care providers a concern for alleviating disease. At the same time, recreational therapy's expanded view of health allows the profession to do more.

Recreational therapists go beyond the traditional medical model in that they have concern for the whole person, not just the disease. Recreational therapists strive to facilitate the highest levels of everyday functioning possible physiologically, psychologically, and socially for its clients.

Carl Rogers: The Grandfather of Recreational Therapy

Carl Rogers is known as the father of client-centered therapy (later termed person-centered therapy). I think a case can be made that recreational therapy should grant Rogers the status of being its grandfather because his approach has seemingly had a tremendous impact on recreational therapy.

Carl Rogers rejected the medical model that imposed expert views on clients. He also took a humanistic perspective that rejected the deterministic psychoanalytic and behavioral approaches. Instead of following these mechanistic approaches, Rogers embraced an approach that was marked by three significant elements.

The first of these elements was an accepting approach with his clients in psychological distress. This element was exemplified by displaying a positive, warm, and accepting attitude toward the client. He labeled this "unconditional positive regard."

Rogers' second element was "empathetic understanding." By this he meant that therapists need to experience a full understanding of their client's private world. Additionally, therapists need to convey to clients that they possess empathy toward their clients.

The final element reflected in Rogers' client-centered approach was being genuine with clients or "congruence." Being congruent to Rogers meant the therapist was himself or herself. There was no façade or false front put up by the therapist (Rogers, 1961).

At the core of the humanistic theory that served as a foundation for Rogers' approaches to therapy is the belief that people possess a natural tendency toward self-actualization. The humanistic theory further rested on the notion that people should have the freedom to be self-determining, to make choices about what was best for them. Thus, the idea of giving clients as much independence as possible became a central part of the humanistic perspective.

The humanistic perspective of Rogers viewed persons holistically. By being viewed holistically, people were seen as being more than the sum of their parts and in the context of their relationships with others and their environments. People were further seen to be social beings who have a strong need to belong and to feel valued.

The notion that people are social beings led Rogers to emphasize the therapeutic relationship that focused on the three elements of "unconditional positive regard," "empathetic understanding," and "congruence" discussed earlier. Rogers saw the therapeutic relationship as a means to promote clients' growth so they might deal not only with their presenting problem but prepare to deal with future problems as well (Cain, 2002).

Do the concepts expressed in Rogers' humanistic perspective sound familiar to you? Do his concepts fit into your view of recreational therapy? My guess is that they do.

I would go so far as to state that Rogers has had a profound impact on recreational therapy. I know that personally Rogers' views have made an enormous impression on me and have influenced my approach to recreational therapy. Let me discuss concepts from Rogers and his humanistic perspective that I believe have affected not only my view but the views of recreational therapists everywhere.

The core concept of clients possessing an inherent tendency for personal growth and development seems to me to be a concept embodied in the practice of recreational therapy. This central notion from humanistic theory has influenced recreational therapists to offer their clients the freedom to exercise their rights to make responsible, self-determined choices so they can maintain as much independence as possible within their treatment and rehabilitation.

The concept of employing a holistic approach is likewise something embraced by recreational therapists. Our clients are seen as more than the sum of their parts. This holistic perspective has led recreational therapists toward a biopsychosocial view of health in which they see the biological, psychological, and social aspects of health as being paramount. Isn't this holistic approach a central element in recreational therapy? I think it is.

Another concept taken directly from Rogers and his humanistic perspective is that of the social nature of human beings that is reflected in their desire to belong and to feel valued. Certainly recreation is a social enterprise in which recreational therapists develop therapeutic relationships with clients and through which clients meet their needs for belonging and enhancing their sense of self.

An extension of this social view is that, like Rogers, recreational therapists typically provide their clients with a warm, positive, accepting, and nonjudgmental atmosphere within recreational therapy programs. A part of this atmosphere is displaying an empathetic understanding toward clients that is genuine and without pretensions. Recreational therapists don't put up false fronts. Their demeanor is one of not trying to be better than their clients but one of being on the same level as their clients and, in fact, being partners with clients by joining with them in their task of protecting or promoting their health.

Finally, I believe that recreational therapists strive to help their clients to not only meet their presenting problems but to grow so that they may be prepared to meet future problems as well. Recreational therapists go beyond immediate treatment concerns to help their clients to develop themselves to the fullest by using a wellness or health promotion perspective.

I know that I have liked Rogers' client-centered approach from the time I came to understand it. His ideas just seem to have a wonderful fit with recreational therapy. It also could be that I am drawn to Rogers partly because I share his Midwestern roots. Born in Oak Park, Illinois (in 1902), Rogers was a "Midwestern guy" and a "Big 10 guy," having held faculty positions at Ohio State and the University of Wisconsin (Hall, 1997).

It seems obvious to me that Carl Rogers has had a significant impact on the practice of recreational therapy and that his influence will always live on through recreational therapy practice. That is why I term Carl Rogers to be "the grandfather" of recreational therapy.

As a footnote to this chapter on the impact of Rogers on recreational therapy, I do wish to be clear that, in addition to Rogers, other therapists and theories have also impacted on recreational therapy. Influences have come from any number of approaches, including psychoanalytic, behavioral, cognitive behavioral, and positive psychology perspectives. As I have discussed in my book *Therapeutic Recreation: Processes and Techniques* (Austin, 2009), recreational therapy is eclectic. Because of Rogers' profound impact on our profession, I do believe he merits special consideration.

Positive Psychology and Recreational Therapy

Closely related to the humanistic psychology of Rogers discussed in the previous lesson is the more modern approach termed positive psychology. As the name implies, positive psychology takes a positive perspective of human beings. For example, like the humanistic approach, positive psychology views all people, with and without disabilities, as possessing a tendency to grow toward their optimal levels of health. Also, like the humanistic approach, positive psychology's approach is one that sees focusing on positive things as one of the best means to help those who are suffering from distress. Finally, both the humanistic and positive psychology approaches are strength-based, focusing on human strengths, not weaknesses.

One feature that sets positive psychology apart from humanistic psychology, however, is that it focuses strictly on a scientific approach. Positive psychology emphasizes a scientific basis by resting its body of knowledge solely upon empirical evidence (Austin, 2009).

Positive psychology only gained its foothold at the beginning of the 21st Century. Therefore, it is still relatively new and many in recreational therapy are just now becoming familiar with it. As it becomes better known, I predict positive psychology will strongly influence the practice of recreational therapy.

As a matter of fact, it seems to me that positive psychology will join with humanistic psychology in forming a solid theoretical foundation for recreational therapy practice. I say this because positive psychology just seems to have a wonderful fit with what we have traditionally done in recreational therapy.

For instance, positive psychologists Linley and Stephen (2004) have written that those using positive psychology "work both to alleviate distress and to promote optimal functioning" (p. 6). Isn't alleviating distress and promoting optimal functioning exactly what recreational therapists have traditionally striven to provide their clients, while using a positive approach emphasizing the fun and mastery that accompany recreation and leisure experiences?

But what is this thing called positive psychology? Perhaps the best way to begin to describe it is to discuss what have been termed its three pillars.

Martin Seligman, the "father" of positive psychology, has described the three pillars. He has written: "First is the study of positive emotion. Second is the study of positive traits, foremost among them the strengths and virtues, but also the 'abilities' such as intelligence and athleticism. Third is the study of the positive institutions, such as democracy, strong families, and free inquiry, that support the virtues, which in turn support positive emotions" (Seligman, 2002, p. ix).

What are positive emotions that represent the first pillar of positive psychology? Positive emotions encompass past emotional experiences (such as contentment and satisfaction), current emotional experiences (such as happiness and flow), and anticipated emotional experiences (such as hope and optimism) (Seligman, 2002).

Fredrickson's (2001) Broaden-and-Build Theory of Positive Emotion is arguably the leading positive psychology theory dealing with positive emotion. The Broaden-and-Build Theory sees positive emotions as having the effect of releasing people to broaden their thoughts and actions. This permits them to feel free to take more risks or to challenge or stretch themselves. In short, their positive emotions free them up or open them up to new ways to think or behave.

Stop and think about yourself. When you are happy and feeling good about yourself and the world, are you much more optimistic and risk taking than when you are down in the dumps? Of course you are. We all are. That is human nature.

Positive emotions, by making people receptive to new thinking and behaving, then allow them to build strengths that they would not have without being freed up. So positive emotions broaden people (i.e., open them up to new thoughts and actions) so that they may try out new ways of thinking or behaving that can lead them to build their skills and abilities.

Positive emotions also have the "side effect" of serving as antidotes for the effects of negative emotions that can linger. Fredrickson (2001) refers to good feelings negating the lingering effects of negative emotions as the "undoing hypothesis."

In transferring Fredrickson's theory to recreational therapy, we can see that the positive emotions experienced in recreational therapy can open clients up to new experiences through which they can overcome current problems and develop themselves for the future. At the same time, the experiencing of good feelings can help clients to get rid of negative feelings. Thus, you can see that the positive psychology's first pillar of positive emotions provides a strong theoretical basis for recreational therapy.

I think it is important for recreational therapists to recognize that the positive emotions they help their clients to achieve represent far more than "fun" or "feel good" experiences. The positive feelings brought about in recreation and leisure activities are not an end, but means to an end. This is because positive emotional experiences in activities open doors for clients, doors that lead to help clients to reach their goals of achieving health and well-being.

Biswas-Diener and Dean (2007) clearly expressed the importance of positive emotions to recreational therapy clients when they exclaimed: "Foul moods can sap energy from clients and interfere with good relationships while positivity offers the best possible chance for success. It is important that you consider happiness and other positive emotions as more than a desirable finish line. Positivity, research shows, is a vital resource that helps clients to reach their goals" (p. 72).

The second of the three pillars of positive psychology is positive traits or strengths. Positive traits or strengths include the athletic and intellectual abilities we inherit, as well as the virtues or moral traits we develop. Of course, both inherited and cultivated traits have to be developed. The development of these human potentials produce feelings of happiness and well-being in people.

Recreational therapy can help clients to identify and develop positive traits or strengths that can be used to overcome problems clients experience. The development of positive traits or strengths can also produce feelings of pride, mastery, and self-fulfillment in clients.

Recreational therapists have long assessed their clients to determine strengths and abilities they possess. Then these strengths and abilities have served as the focal point for interventions to assist clients to overcome threats to health. In fact, it may be said that recreational therapists perhaps preceded positive psychologists in embracing the notion that clients' strengths and abilities can become the focus of a strength-based approach to treatment and rehabilitation.

The third pillar is that of positive institutions. Positive institutions are environmental influences that can impact positively on the development of people's traits or strengths. Environmental influences relate to two areas of recreational therapy.

One area of environmental influence is that of the recreational therapist providing the best type of environment to support interventions. An example of a positive institution could be an outdoor adventure program that provides the right amount of challenge for the individual so that the environment fosters growth in the person's positive traits or strengths.

Thus, within recreational therapy, interventions need to transpire in environments that are positive so that they foster growth in client traits and strengths. Of course, the development of traits or strengths results in clients experiencing positive emotions.

A second area of environmental influence within recreational therapy is that of taking into account how the client's environment has affected him or her in the past and how changing the client's environment may affect the client in the future. We in recreational therapy have perhaps given the least attention to this aspect of positive institutions.

It seems to me that we have often neglected our clients' environments when considering our clients' problems. Instead of examining our clients' environments to determine how they may be improved to make them more positive, we have typically asked our individual clients to change themselves in order to adjust to their environments.

Thus, positive psychology provides a good reminder to recreational therapists that we need to give consideration to assessing clients' environments as well as their needs and strengths. It may be that we need to seek changes in the client's environment rather than changes in the client (Austin, 2009).

As recreational therapists, we must look at both of these aspects of positive institutions. As previously indicated, as recreational therapists we need to closely examine the environments in which we deliver our programs and activities to assure they foster positive emotions and develop clients' positive traits.

Additionally, we need to examine the environments from which our clients come so we can attempt to make those environments positive ones that support clients if they have not been positive in the past. Therefore, sometimes recreational therapists must work to change the client's environment, rather than change the client.

So there you have it. Positive psychology's three pillars of positive emotion, positive traits, and positive institutions seem to have a wonderful fit with what we do in recreational therapy. What do you think?

Freud and Skinner Weren't Completely Wrong

Freud's psychoanalytic theory has today lost favor among most therapists. Freud's view that we humans are controlled by unconscious instinctual forces has been almost completely dismissed.

To a lesser degree, the behavioral approach has also lost its position as a major force within the therapy community. It is the work of the late Indiana and Harvard psychologist B.F. Skinner in the area of external reinforcement that is perhaps most closely associated with behavior therapy and behavior modification. Skinner and other behaviorists believed that the environment played the key role in influencing people's behavior.

Psychoanalysis was first on the scene. It was the dominant theoretical perspective when I first worked in mental health in the early 1960s. Behaviorism followed. Behavioral approaches were beginning to become popular in psychiatric settings about the time I left practice to do my Ph.D. in the late 1960s.

With the emergence of humanistic psychology, both psychoanalytic theory and behaviorism were roundly criticized. Freud's biological determinism and the behaviorists' environmental determinism were both viewed by humanistic psychologists to be mechanistic approaches that did not account for people's desire to be self-aware and self-directed.

Although psychoanalysis is far from the dominant theoretical perspective it once was, some ideas from Freud still have useful applications in recreational therapy practice. For example, recreational therapists should realize that unconscious motivation may in fact affect their clients' behaviors. Also, recreational therapists need to recognize that clients often employ the defense mechanisms described by Freud as means to protect their self-concepts. Finally, recreational therapists should recognize that events during clients' developmental years may affect them as adults.

There are also concepts to be learned from Skinner and the behaviorists. Recreational therapists need to understand the idea of reinforcement, for example, because their clients' behaviors will be affected by the consequences of their behaviors. If clients find their behaviors to be rewarded, they are likely to repeat them. Similarly, if behaviors are not rewarded, they will be less likely to be repeated. Knowing how reinforcers influence client behavior can be highly useful to understanding reward systems that surround and influence client behaviors. Recreational therapists can also employ behavior modification techniques, such as reinforcing desirable behaviors, when striving to treat discrete behaviors. Finally, behavior modification procedures such as shaping, modeling, prompting, fading, time-out, and behavioral contracts may have application in recreational therapy (See Austin, 2009, for further information on the psychoanalytic and behavioral approaches).

I once had a professor who used the expression "throwing the baby out with the bath water." I think that expression is applicable when thinking about ideas that can be taken from the psychology of Freud and Skinner. While the paradigms of Freud and Skinner no longer have the standing they once enjoyed, there certainly are concepts that can be drawn from them for application in recreational therapy.

The New Recreational Therapist's Anxiety in Group Leadership

I can recall as a young recreational therapist having a problem in my activity leadership. I was far too concerned with myself and how I would "look" when leading activities. I was worried first about myself and about appearing incompetent, rather than focusing on the outcomes that my clients might derive from taking part.

I think there are a couple of lessons that come out of my experience. The first is that in any new situation most of us feel insecure. Feeling insecure can be anxiety provoking. Anxiety can make us self-focused as we try to protect our egos. We can become self-absorbed. I was no doubt feeling very insecure and anxious when I lead my first groups.

The second lesson is that my experience turned out to be not unusual. Much to my personal relief, I discovered that most emerging therapists are far too self-concerned when they initially begin to practice. The majority of therapists go through a phase when they are too self-centered prior to gaining the experiences they need to become secure in their abilities.

Anxiety is to be expected when we are thrust into new situations. In fact, a little anxiety is probably a good thing in that it gets us "up" for performing in our new role. It is only when our anxiety becomes too strong that it produces a debilitating effect that interferes with our functioning.

Emerging recreational therapists will likely experience insecurity and anxiety when initially leading groups. If this happens, a healthy reaction would be admitting to your anxiety and talking with others about it. A conference with your clinical supervisor would be a good time to divulge your feelings. In doing so, you will probably discover that your clinical supervisor suffered similar feelings when he or she first assumed leadership responsibilities.

Recreational Therapy Groups Offer Participants Numerous Benefits

Some recreational therapy services are delivered by recreational therapists to clients in one-to-one therapy situations. Most recreational therapy, however, is done in groups with one or two recreational therapist providing leadership for a group.

You may be asking yourself why recreational therapy programs are typically delivered in group situations. The most obvious answer is that it is more economical to serve several clients at one time than to see them separately. This is true, but I think the reason for the delivery of so many group programs in recreational therapy goes beyond pure economics.

People join groups for a variety of specific reasons. Of course, the overriding reason is that they have a need that they wish to meet through their participation in the group. Thus, groups offer outcomes to people that they cannot gain in one-on-one therapy.

Like others, our clients also have specific outcomes they are seeking from their membership in recreational therapy groups. And, of course, these outcomes are related to the needs they wish to meet.

What are some outcomes that clients can achieve in recreational therapy groups? It seems to me that there are two obvious outcomes for clients in our groups.

One outcome is that our groups offer clients a way to meet their need to belong. Groups meet a basic need of clients by providing a feeling of belonging. This is particularly true when members begin to "bond" with one another. A dynamic in the bonding process is that members often discover that others suffer from similar problems as they do. Thus, our clients do not feel alone in having a problem. This can be reassuring to them.

The other obvious outcome for clients who participate in recreational therapy groups is being in a supportive environment. Recreational therapy groups typically provide a warm, accepting atmosphere in which the leader and group members will be sympathetic toward the problems experienced by others in the group. Thus, recreational therapy groups tend to provide members with social support.

My former colleague, professor Bryan McCormick of Indiana University, has studied clients with severe and persistent mental illness who reside in a large city in the Midwest. In conversations with Bryan, I recall he told me that the mentally ill men that he talked with often reported having few friends. They simply had never developed a close group of friends that they belonged to. Of course, because they did not belong to a group they lacked the social support that they might have found through their group membership.

These men with chronic mental illness needed to become involved in groups to meet their needs to belong, which in turn, would likely lead them to feel a level of social support.

One thing that handicapped these men was their lack of social skills, including recreational skills. Recreational skills can play a large part of bonding with others. People interact around a game or sport that they share, such as playing cards or even being a baseball fan. Without the skills to relate positively with others, the men experienced difficulties in forming relationships.

The account of the men in Professor McCormick's research reminds me of a couple of other outcomes that recreational therapy groups often offer clients. One is that participants can learn social skills, including recreational skills, within recreational therapy groups. Another related outcome is that recreational therapy groups offer members opportunities to practice and hone their social skills that are critical to their ability to build and sustain relationships with others.

Other possible outcomes from groups include these benefits: having the opportunity to receive advice or suggestions from other group members; learning new behaviors from modeling after the leader or other members of the group; learning new roles they may take within a group; experiencing a closeness with others that allows the person to open up to others; learning to interact with diverse individuals; finding out how others interpret behaviors; and enjoying success and gaining encouragement from others.

There are times when clients are not ready for group experiences. For instance, a client might be too fragile to benefit from group participation or group participation might make them too anxious when they initially become a client.

For more information on these advantages and disadvantages of participation in recreational therapy groups you may wish to see Table 7.2 on pages 327 and 328 in my book (Austin, 2009) *Therapeutic Recreation: Processes and Techniques*. Those who wish to read more about social support are encouraged to read Professor McCormick's (2002) chapter titled "Social Support in Therapeutic Recreation" in the book titled *Conceptual Foundations for Therapeutic Recreation* (Austin, Dattilo, & McCormick, 2002).

Group Processing Should Be Regularly Completed with RT Groups

I can recall visiting one of our university recreational therapy students who was completing her major internship at a state psychiatric hospital in Oregon. On the particular day that I observed the student intern, she was working with a group of men who were mentally disabled, as well as mentally ill.

The activity this group of men was engaged in was that of making collages. The men went through old magazines in which they found pictures that represented something they wished for themselves. They cut out these pictures and pasted them together, each building his own collage out of the pictures he had selected.

When the men had completed their collages, each showed his to the other men in the group as well as to student intern. As they did, each explained his collage and how it represented something he wanted for himself. I can recall one particular man whose collage included a picture of a champion swimmer. This man discussed how he, like the pictured swimmer, would like to get into top shape physically.

Following each man's interpretation of his collage to the group the recreational therapy intern asked him to relate his collage to specific goals in his treatment plan. To my total surprise, this each man was able to do. For example, the fellow who talked about wanting to get into better shape related this desire to his treatment plan that included improving his physical condition.

I sat there watching this in amazement. I had never expected our student intern to be able to debrief any group, let along one composed of men who were both mentally retarded and mentally ill! Nor did I ever expect that this particular group of men would have little difficulty in participating in the debriefing process that culminated in their relating the activity to their individual treatment plans.

Until I had my eyes opened by viewing debriefing being used with that group of hospitalized men, I had always thought of group processing as something only done with intellectually gifted high school or college students in an adventure therapy program or well educated adults undergoing treatment in a private psychiatric hospital. The experience of observing our undergraduate recreational therapy intern using group processing so skillfully with this group of men was a mind-altering experience, to say the least.

Having seen this for myself, I could understand how group processing could be used with almost any type of client in almost any recreational therapy setting. Yet even today, I believe most recreational therapists (wrongly) associate group processing largely with groups of bright clients who discuss their participation after taking part in games, icebreakers, team-building exercises, or adventure therapy programs.

My experience in observing our intern displayed to me that group processing can be used by recreational therapists with almost any group of clients and in virtually any group activity. I have come to believe that group processing should be regularly completed with all recreational therapy groups.

I suppose for those readers not acquainted with group processing that I should discuss more specifically what is meant by it. Group processing is a way to help group members learn from their direct experiences of participating in an activity. In doing a group activity, discussing the dynamics of what went on, and then applying this learning to their everyday lives, people experience experiential learning through their direct participation.

Group processing then involves means of allowing group members to gain self-awareness from their participation in group activities. Such self-awareness includes insights into areas such as the participants' interaction patterns, thought processes, attitudes, and values.

The expectation is that insights gained from group members' participation can be extended beyond the group in which they are revealed. It is the intent of leaders conducting group processing that members translate what they have learned from their group participation to their everyday lives.

Recreational therapists when hearing the term "group processing" sometimes equate it only with debriefing group members following their participation in an activity. The equating of the terms "group processing" and "debriefing" may be because one of the early adopted forms of group processing in recreational therapy was a debriefing framework. This was one introduced by Schoel, Prouty, and Radcliffe in their adventure counseling book published in 1988. The book employed the questions of: "What?," "So What?," and "Now What?" in the participants' discussion of an activity in which they had taken part.

Today debriefing probably remains the most used form of group processing but other types of group processing are employed as well. These include techniques such as frontloading (where therapists focus the awareness of group members on relevant issues prior to beginning the activity), feedback (where therapists offer feedback to members about something that has just happened in the activity), and metaphors (a figure of speech in which something is used as a symbol by therapists to represent something else) (Austin, 2009).

Recreational therapists can use any group processing technique to facilitate the transfer of client learning from the activity to their real world lives. It is important to process activities because otherwise clients may not link their experiences from their group participation to their individual lives. Many hold that without group processing in recreational therapy few therapeutic benefits will likely be derived by clients taking part in group recreation experiences.

Chapter 22

Techniques When Clients Don't Participate in Group Discussions

As a university instructor, I had times when the students in my classes did not participate in the class discussion. As a young instructor, I would often talk myself when my students did not enter into the discussion in order to fill in the "dead space." (By the way, filling in the silence is definitely not a good idea. It is much better to let others fill in silence. In fact, silence can be used as a technique to encourage discussion.) Thank goodness I eventually learned ways to stimulate my students' discussion on days they were reluctant to participate.

As in the university classroom, there will be times when members of recreational therapy groups for one reason or another just do not enter into group discussion. What can the recreational therapist do when this occurs?

The same techniques that work to stimulate discussions in the university classroom seem to transfer well to therapy groups. One of these is eye contact. The group leader can look directly at a member of the group and even nod at that individual. If the person doesn't respond, the leader may follow up by asking that individual, "What do you think, Mary?"

Another technique is for the leader to ask a quiet member of the group if he or she agrees with what was said. "Do you think that is right, Jack?' the leader might say. The respondent is not forced into offering a long answer, as the individual is only asked to agree or disagree. A related technique is to ask a quiet member to share his or her thoughts about the topic under consideration. In either case the leader should not be confrontational so the quiet respondent doesn't feel he or she has been put on the spot.

Another way to encourage discussion is to tell members of the group that you will be randomly calling on them during the discussion. If a leader uses this approach, it is a good idea to have a list of participants in front of him or her so it is obvious to those in the group that they are being selected at random from the list.

Whenever asking a group member for a response it is important to make sure you give them an adequate amount of time to respond. I can recall reading a study completed years ago that found that the average classroom teacher only allows two or three seconds for a student to respond before asking another student. This is simply not enough time for some people to form their thoughts and then to speak. To be sure I gave my students enough time, I would sometimes count to 10 in my head before either repeating the question in other words than I had initially posed it or asking another student to answer.

A final technique to spur group discussion is to go around the circle, asking each member of the group to take a turn in voicing his or her opinion. This is a democratic approach but one that may force some quiet group members to speak before they are really ready to take part, leading them to feel embarrassed or ill at ease.

Get a Background in Group Dynamics, Because You'll Need It

Something I can recall from my days as a young recreational therapist was that things happened in the groups I ran that I simply didn't understand. This was extremely disconcerting, because I felt responsible for everything that happened in my groups, and yet sometimes I couldn't comprehend what was going on, let alone know how to respond to what was happening.

I can remember thinking, "After all, these are my groups. I've been given the leadership responsibility for them. So I need to be to control and direct my groups so that the goals for the groups are met." And yet, many times in my groups, things didn't go at all as I anticipated or desired.

A character from an old TV show that my family watched religiously when I was growing up used to regularly exclaim when faced with a dilemma, "What a revolting development this is!" These were my often my exact sentiments as I struggled to be in command of "my groups." (I actually considered them "my groups" rather than the members' groups. In my mind, the groups were mine to control in ways that would make the members "act right.")

Having never studied group dynamics at the time, I had no idea that groups typically go through stages. Had I known this, I would have better understood some of the things that went on in my groups.

For example, I didn't understand when members were experiencing a difficult time forming together into a unit. And so, being ignorant of group dynamics, I did nothing to facilitate members of my groups developing a sense of groupness.

Nor did I realize it was a natural occurrence for members to wish to assume more leadership for the group as time went on. And so, again being ignorant of group dynamics, I fought members for leadership because I thought that it was my job to lead the group and, of course, they got angry at me for not allowing them to have more power.

Many things that happened in my groups those many years ago seem obvious to me now, but at the time I didn't have a clue. I am relating this to you to impress upon you the tremendous importance of gaining a strong background in group processes, because you will need all the information you can gain about groups when you work with recreational therapy groups.

Without knowing the basics of group dynamics, you will be putting yourself and your clients in peril. Know, for example, that facilitating recreational therapy groups will demand that you start your work long before the first group meeting by doing pregroup planning. You will have to develop a protocol that will cover: (a) Determining exactly why the group needs to be formed; (b) Formulating general objectives for the group (c) Deciding the group size, the length of group sessions, and whether the group will be open to adding new members or if it will be closed to new members; (d) Determining the characteristics of clients in your target group; and (e) Considering how you will evaluate the group. All these things need to be well thought out in planning for a group.

Then be sure you know the normal group stages and roles and functions you will need to assume in facilitating a group at each stage in the group's development. For instance, in the early sessions in the initial stage of group development, members will have acceptance concerns—how others see them and how they fit into the group. So at this time, you need to not only be aware that your group is going through this initial stage but how you will help members to reduce anxiety, feel more comfortable, and begin to feel a part of the group. It will be your role to build a climate of acceptance and trust within your group.

In sum, I hope you will learn from my personal shortcoming of not having been properly prepared to assume leadership of recreational therapy groups. It is critical if you are going to do recreational therapy that you have solid understanding of group dynamics and what you will need to do to facilitate your groups at each stage.

By the way, the reason for my lack of preparation was that in the early years, when the field of recreational therapy was still in the process of professionalization, the opportunities for professional preparation were just beginning. Few universities offered curricula in recreational therapy. Thank goodness, today's recreational therapists are generally much better prepared than were we back in the 1960s.

One thing, however, has not changed since I was a young recreational therapist. That is that young professionals can learn much from seasoned practitioners.

When I was a young professional, I learned most of what I knew from veteran staff who had been working at the hospital for years. As an emerging professional, you have had the advantage of having taken courses that provide a solid foundation for practice. Yet I can tell you that one of the best ways for you to learn how to work with groups is to serve as a co-leader with a seasoned recreational therapist. I would urge you to find a skilled clinician and to learn about group work from that senior person.

Recreational Therapists are Models for Clients

Do you recall when growing up how you would try to act like those whom you admired? I can recall when I was in junior high school that I tried to walk in the same manner as "Jo Jo" Shires, who was a star athlete at the local college.

Jo Jo ran the dashes on the track team and was a wide receiver on the football team. Jo Jo was a small man (probably 5' 8" or so), but he was exceptionally fast. He was a joy to watch as an athlete and he would pay attention to me. When I would hang around his team practices, he would say, "hi" to me or ask me how I was doing. Jo Jo quickly became my boyhood idol.

Because Jo Jo was fast, he always seemed to move briskly. I can recall watching him walking across campus with his arms and legs swinging really fast. Tall for my age of 12 or 13, my natural gate might have been described as slow and gangly. But because I was so enamored by Jo Jo, I tried to walk like him. I must have looked pretty silly as I walked, frantically pumping my arms and moving my hips as fast as I could go. Needless to say, I was probably the only one who recognized any similarity between my walking form and that of Jo Jo!

I tell this story because it reflects that we tend to imitate those who we like or admire. Even today, when I examine my own behavior, I must admit that while I no longer try to walk like Jo Jo, I occasionally try to dress like Phil Mickelson (perhaps with the false hope that by imitating Phil my golf game will improve).

Recreational therapists need to display to their clients positive ways to behave. This is because clients often become close to their recreational therapists, whom they like and admire. Because of this relationship, clients are apt to wish to model the behaviors of their recreational therapists.

Because our personal role modeling can affect our clients, we need to monitor our behaviors to be sure we know what we are exhibiting to our clients. Such self-examination is particularly important for emerging recreational therapists so they are aware of the behaviors they are presenting to clients.

Is Recreational Therapy an Art or a Science, or Both?

You, as a recreational therapist, will have to determine your personal approach to recreational therapy. Today there is no one accepted approach to recreational therapy. By approach, I mean an idealized notion, worldview, or explanation that serves as a theoretical basis for practice. Our approaches assist us to understand how people and their environments exist and therefore give us ways and means to follow in practice.

Some see recreational therapy through the eyes of science. They believe only in evidence-based practice with its foundations in science. Others perceive recreational therapy to be more of an art form. They take a humane view that focuses on the individual client and his or her needs and emotions. Still others believe recreational therapy is both an art and a science. They draw on both the perspectives of those who see recreational therapy as an art and those who take a scientific approach.

Because there exists no one approach to recreational therapy practice in the United States or Canada, each recreational therapist must look at his or her profession as it exists and decide for himself or herself whether recreational therapy is an art, a science, or a combination of the two.

This lesson takes a broad perspective in examining whether the profession of recreational therapy is an art or science, or a combination. Hopefully, what I present will help you to make a determination as to your personal perspective on the art and science of recreational therapy. Of course, as I have done in other lessons in this book, I will share my personal perspective within this lesson.

Let's examine the scientific approach first. Those who take a scientific approach tend to follow a strict biomedical model. These individuals take an organic view. They look at clients as a collection of parts, much like a machine (Marcum, 2008).

When I think of the scientific approach, thoughts of colleagues who work in physical rehabilitation initially come to mind. Recreational therapists who work in physical rehabilitation tend to use terms such as "functional ability" to describe client outcomes. They seem to care primarily about improvement in their clients' functioning abilities such as a client's range of motion, a client's ability to transfer from their wheelchair to a chair, car, boat, or some other object, or a client's abilities to negotiate the environment in his or her wheelchair while using community facilities such as restaurants or theaters. Their concern seems to be almost singly directed at the functional status of clients.

Those who follow a strict scientific approach are most concerned with the "facts." They ask exactly what measurable progress can be made or will be made in the client's abilities. Marcum (2008) has stated that the scientifically based biomedical approach has produced a number of successful outcomes in the treatment and rehabilitation of clients with a variety of diseases and disorders. He has warned, however, it may not take into consideration what the client is experiencing and what is important to the client.

Those who favor viewing recreational therapy as an art take a more holistic approach. They tend to subscribe to a broad biopsychosocial approach. They perceive individuals' bodies, minds, and social environments each play a role in diseases and disorders, as well as in clients' treatment and rehabilitation programs (Marcum, 2008).

When I think about recreational therapy as an art, I think of those in mental health who take into consideration what clients are experiencing, along with the clients' values and preferences. Their broad-based approach has concern for the biological, psychological, and social aspects of each individual client.

Recreational therapists who approach their work as an art take a very personal approach with clients. Their clinical interactions are perceived by them to play a significant role, so they place great emphasis on the healing relationship. In short, those who subscribe to recreational therapy as an art are largely concerned with the total therapeutic milieu in caring for each client as a unique individual.

My personal view is that recreational therapy is both an art and a science. I believe recreational therapists should apply science by following evidence-based practice (EBP). I hope you will read the lesson in this book in which I discuss EBP. At the same time, our clients, to me, are far more than their physical or chemical states. They are total beings. Therefore, the traditional humanistic and client-centered approach that has long been a part of recreational therapy demands an artful approach in delivering recreational therapy services.

In this book, I have written about the importance of the therapist/client relationship. I have gone so far to proclaim the therapeutic relationship is at the heart of recreational therapy. I have discussed the importance of therapeutic communications in maintaining healthy helping relationships. I've also stated how the holistic approach has become a vital part of recreational therapy delivery, and I've written of helping clients to assume an optimal amount of control as we assist them in their quests for independence. All of these elements of recreational therapy practice point to the art of recreational therapy.

What is your personal approach to recreational therapy? Do you favor a scientific approach or an approach that sees recreational therapy as an art? Or do you, as I do, perceive recreational therapy as both an art and a science? No matter our views, both you and I can profit from wisdom drawn from a book on medicine and philosophy by Johansson and Lynoe (2008). These authors stated:

"Fallibilism implies tolerance. Everyone needs to hear criticism of his (or her) views in order to keep them valid, and such an insight might ground some tolerance. But as soon as one acknowledges the possibility that one may be wrong—partly or wholly—one has to become much more tolerant. Why? Because then criticism might be needed in order for oneself to be able to improve one's views. Tolerance is necessary not only in religion and political matters, but also in scientific and philosophical." (p. 5)

Enthusiasm

Recreational therapists are characterized by enthusiasm. They are typically outgoing individuals full of enthusiasm for what they do. This enthusiasm is displayed by the positive, energetic approach they bring to the activities in which they engage their clients.

I once asked one of my entering graduate students why she had come back to the university to study recreational therapy. The student answered that while she had been a hospital dietitian she had observed that the only employees at her hospital that really seemed to enjoy their jobs were the recreational therapists. She said she wanted return to school to be able to join a profession where those in it had fun at what they did.

I think the "gung-ho" attitude typical of recreational therapists is primarily because they really like their work and maintain a fervent belief in what they do. They truly believe that what they do is important and can make a significant difference in the lives of those they serve.

Emerging recreational therapists learn it is important not only to be engaged with their profession but to display to others their enthusiasm for what they are doing. If recreational therapists are enthusiastic, it is more likely their clients will become energized. The old saying that "enthusiasm is catching" seems to often hold true for the clients of recreational therapists.

On the other hand, emerging recreational therapists need to also come to understand that clients at first may not be enthusiastic participants in recreational therapy programs. In fact, emerging recreational therapists will be greatly disappointed if they think their clients will initially be "naturally" enthusiastic.

Clients have to be given something to become enthusiastic about. Instead of expecting enthusiasm, recreational therapists should be pleased when clients show enthusiasm!

A universal characteristic of clients I have observed is that, no matter what their specific health concern is, they tend to lack feeling in control over their situations. I have written elsewhere (Austin, 2002b) about how mental well-being is largely defined by the levels of control people have over their thoughts, feelings, and behaviors. Examples of obvious mental health problems involving clients' lack of personal control include stress and anxiety disorders, drug and alcohol addictions, and depression.

In that same 2002 piece, I discussed how a sense of control relates to people's adaptations to physical disorders. Persons who are not optimistic, who lack a sense of control, tend to be those who experience anxiety and depression. At the extreme are people with such a low sense of control they develop feelings of helplessness and succumb to their illnesses much more readily than those with higher perceived control.

Because it is generally important for people to maintain a sense of control, experiencing a lack of control can be demoralizing. Unfortunately, demoralization is a too common characteristic of our clients.

Is it then any surprise that clients experiencing demoralization do not express enthusiasm for participation in recreational therapy programs? Clients must be given reasons to become enthusiastic participants.

I do not believe that there is any group of helping professionals better than naturally enthusiastic recreational therapists at helping clients enhance feelings of control, feelings which ultimately result in greater client engagement in programs. This result comes about   because gains in feelings of control are accompanied by diminished feelings of demoralization. These heightened feelings of control and diminished feedings of demoralization lead clients toward an "I can" attitude that produces enthusiastic participants.

I believe a factor in the process of clients regaining control and diminishing demoralization is the fact that recreational therapists offer their clients the antithesis of a controlling environment. A value held by recreational therapists is to strive to leave as much control as possible with their clients by letting them make choices regarding programs and activities.

Recreational therapy is also about providing clients with opportunities to use their strengths in doing things they enjoy. This participation allows clients to achieve success and mastery-experiences that bring about positive emotions and help build feelings of self-efficacy.

Finally, recreational therapy fosters safe, supportive environments. Social support can provide clients with comfort and relief from stress, which may be helpful to clients regaining personal control. As a part of establishing a safe, supportive environment recreational therapists offer clients direct emotional support by being warm and friendly toward clients and by projecting optimistic attitudes. Recreational therapists bring infectious energy, enthusiasm, and positivism.

This, of course, doesn't mean that recreational therapists are "Pollyannaish." Recreational therapists are not foolishly or excessively optimistic. Nor are they saccharine or overly cheerful. Clients easily catch on to such phony behaviors. These behaviors are not a part of the character of sincere recreational therapists.

Clients will start to become enthusiastic participants once they begin to realize that recreational therapy programs offer safe, warm environments in which they can experience autonomy, exercise self-determination, increase feelings of self-efficacy, enhance their moods, and receive social support from enthusiastic recreational therapists. Such positive experiences in recreational therapy tend to move clients from initial feelings of demoralization to feelings of personal control—and from being less than enthusiastic participants to enthusiastically taking part in recreational therapy programs.

Extroversion

When I was doing my first university teaching, one of my students came to me to tell me that she was dropping out of the recreational therapy program because she was not extraverted enough. I can recall being dejected about her decision, because she was one of the brightest of the undergraduate students in our professional preparation program.

Reflecting on my young student's decision to give up recreational therapy because she did not possess an extraverted personality, I have come to the conclusion that she was wise beyond her years. Based on what I now know she made a reasoned decision to change majors because there seems to be a consensus of opinion among those practitioners and educators I have spoken with that the best recreational therapists exhibit high degrees of extroversion (although I don't have any scientific evidence to back up this claim).

There is research to suggest that university recreational therapy students generally are extroverted. In a study of undergraduates in recreational therapy that I helped to conduct (Jin & Austin, 2000) the largest proportion were found to be friendly, socially gregarious, outgoing, and people-oriented extroverts. It appears that these students may have selected recreational therapy because their extroverted personalities were well suited for the profession.

It makes sense that the best recreational therapists would not be shy wallflowers. It helps for recreational therapists to be fun loving, friendly and outgoing, because they regularly need to enthusiastically interact with clients.

This same extroverted personality also is a good one for teachers. Think about it for a moment. Were some of your best teachers enthusiastic individuals who seemed to really enjoy interacting with students? They might even have arrived early for class or stayed after class so that they might chat with you and other students.

Yes, I would hold that for both recreational therapists and teachers exhibiting high levels of extroversion is a very good thing. As an individual who was a recreational therapist early in his career and later became a university professor, I learned that exhibiting extroversion is a needed trait for success in both occupations. And I would have to say that I was able to succeed in both occupations by being extroverted—at least in my "public" persona.

I must confess that it is not my basic nature to be extroverted. My tendency is to be somewhat shy and introverted. It always has been. Even today, I am often not comfortable speaking before groups of people. My face will turn red when I am embarrassed, and I can become tongue-tied when meeting people of importance.

What I am telling you is that even basically introverted people like me can learn to exhibit greater extroversion. While I am sure that I will always have an introverted side to me, I have become much more extroverted.

While my shyness will always be a part of me, I must tell you that I like the extroverted side of me. So if you are somewhat shy but wish to enter the profession of recreational therapy, there is no reason why you can't. But I believe you will have to work at becoming more extroverted if you want to be a successful practitioner.

The "take-home message" is that even if you are a bit shy, you can become a good recreational therapist. You simply have to learn to behave like an extrovert on those occasions when such behavior is required. Of course, if you are a natural extrovert, you are "ahead of the game" when it comes to becoming a good recreational therapist.

Dare to Share

Often practitioners have much to offer others in terms of telling the story of what they do in their practice. Unfortunately, most practitioners seem to be reluctant to give conference presentations or to write for publication. I'm not sure why this is. Perhaps it is because they hold a mistaken belief that they should not stand out or call attention to themselves for fear that others will think that they are better than their colleagues. Perhaps they are just not comfortable in public behaviors such as speaking or writing.

Whatever the reason, it is too bad that practitioners are reluctant to write for publication or to give presentations. Reflective practitioners have much to share about both their successes and failures and such sharing is what a true professional should do.

It has been my experience that university faculty are highly supportive of practitioners who indicate any level of interest in making presentations or authoring papers for publication. A good way for practitioners to begin either doing presentations or writing papers is to seek a faculty member to be a co-presenter or co-author. Faculty members generally are willing to be boosters and mentors for practitioners who wish to share their knowledge with others in the profession by either making presentations or authoring articles.

Another source of support for practitioners is to seek the assistance of nurses, psychologists, medical doctors, and other colleagues at their work place. Many in kindred professionals have rich experiences in giving presentations or writing for publication and are willing to help out a colleague from recreational therapy who wishes to become engaged with their profession by presenting or writing.

The "take-home message" is that those practicing as recreational therapists should exhibit professionalism by sharing with others what they have gained through their experiences in the field. In the spirit of professionalism, these professionals should dare to share.

Learn to Relax

Relaxation techniques are not just for clients. I've learned that it is healthy for me to do some relaxation exercises just before any public behavior, whether it is conducting an activity session, teaching a class, or delivering a talk at a conference.

I think two things are occurring when I complete relaxation exercises before I enter into the event where I want to be mentally prepared to do my best. The first is that I'm consciously demarcating between what I was doing prior to the event that I am about to embark upon and the public performance that I am entering into (e.g., activity session, class, or talk). I am signaling to myself that "it is time to shift gears and prepare to perform at a high level."

The second thing that is occurring when I do my relaxation exercises is that I am physically and mentally reducing feelings of tension. Even the most seasoned veterans feel some level of anxiety prior to being put on the spot by having to lead an activity, teach a class, or give a talk. When I begin my responsibilities, I want to feel relaxed and "ready to go." Feeling physically and mentally relaxed allows me to "clear my head" so that I can give my full attention to the task at hand.

What should you do to relax before you enter into any public behavior? The answer to that question is one that you will discover for yourself. I can tell you what I have found to be effective for me.

One thing I regularly do to prepare myself before teaching class or giving a speech is to practice deep breathing. I just close my eyes and take several slow, deep breaths. Just breathing deeply with my eyes closed helps to put me in a more relaxed state.

Another relaxation technique I've employed just before going to teach a class is to tense and relax muscles in my face and hands. I clamp down my jaws and tighten the muscles of my forehead for just a second and then relax them. After doing this a couple of times, I move to tensing my hands. Several times I clinch my firsts, putting tension in my hands and forearms, and then relax them.

A third technique that I have found to be useful for tension reduction is self-massage. I tend to carry a lot of tension in my neck and shoulders. Therefore, I like to massage my neck and shoulders before leaving my office to go to class. I also shrug my shoulders several times. The self-message and shrugging permits me to experience less tension in my neck and shoulder muscles, allowing me to feel more relaxed.

If you are looking for relaxation techniques that you can try out, you may wish to take a look at those in my book (Austin, 2009). There you will find information such as an extensive list of tips to help you in deep breathing, instruction for progressive muscle relaxation, and techniques for self-massage. You will also find several other approaches to relaxation that I have not mentioned (e.g., yoga, imagery).

If you try out some of the forms of relaxation found in my book, I would hazard a guess that you will learn what techniques work best for you. You will then be able to employ these methods to make you feel more relaxed the next time you have to lead a recreational therapy activity or give a public presentation.

Value Values

When I began my career in recreational therapy, there existed a myth that recreational therapists were "value free." Our personal values were not to play any part in our professional lives.

Of course, as you no doubt would guess, we came to realize that to function value free was impossible. Therefore, today the myth of recreational therapists being value free has vanished. In its place has come an awareness of the importance of knowing our values so we can be very cognizant of the values we hold and the potential for these values to effect our work. Thus, today's recreational therapists must closely examine their value systems so they may be aware of their values and how their values may enter into their professional practice.

Values are the ideals and beliefs that we prize and, as such, they become a vital part of our total being. What we value becomes critical to us, because values are the principles upon which we base our lives. They affect the way we think and act. Our everyday decisions become governed by the values we hold.

Let me provide an example of a basic value. Would you shoplift? Probably not, because of a value you hold against stealing from others. This value you possess governs your decision not to take something that is not yours.

I can even guess some values that are important to you by knowing decisions you have already made. For example, my guess is that you value education because you are studying at a university to prepare yourself to become a recreational therapist. I would also guess that you are a caring person who values helping others or you would not have chosen a helping profession as a career. Am I correct?

Due to the importance of values, we do need to value our values. Every recreational therapist needs to examine his or her values with specific attention to those that may impact upon professional practice. It is particularly important to examine those values that are generally held by those in our profession.

To accomplish an examination of the professional values of recreational therapists may, as they say, be easier said than done. This is because recreational therapy is still an emerging profession, and as such it has not developed an established set of professional values.

I have been so brave (or perhaps brazen!) as to develop what I think are the values possessed by recreational therapists and have published those in my book *Therapeutic Recreation: Processes and Techniques* (Austin, 2009). If you care to, you can go to my book to see the entire list of professional values I have proposed. In this lesson, let me just give you a couple of examples so you can gain a taste for the flavor of them.

One professional value that I believe is held by recreational therapists is that of respecting and promoting client autonomy. This means allowing clients to maintain as much control over their lives as possible, including making informed choices for themselves.

This profession value directly extends to what we do with our clients. For instance, because we value client autonomy, we do not attempt to impose our personal values on clients. Instead, as Corey and Corey (2006) have suggested, we simply expose clients to values with the hope that they will embrace the ones that appeal to them.

Another professional value in my book deals with the intrinsic worth of clients. This value is that each and every client is valued as an individual human being who possesses intrinsic worth and who should be treated with dignity.

This value is one that comes to the forefront today as recreational therapists are apt to serve diverse clients coming from a wide variety of cultural backgrounds. This is why cultural diversity has become an important area of study for all helping professionals, including recreational therapists.

I could go on with listing professional values, but I'm sure you get the idea. Should you want to examine professional values further, I would invite you to read over Figure 5-1 in *Therapeutic Recreation: Processes and Techniques* (Austin, 2009). The title of Figure 5-1 is "Examples of Professional Values of Recreational Therapists."

In sum, what I'm suggesting to you is that your values will have an real impact on what you do as a recreational therapist. Do conduct a self-examination of your personal values, as well as those professional values generally held by recreational therapists. I truly believe such self-examination constitutes a fundamental step to becoming a professional in recreational therapy.

Gaining Cultural Competence

America has become increasingly diverse during my lifetime. It certainly wasn't diverse when I was growing up. At least it wasn't where I grew up in southern Indiana.

The small town where I was raised was mostly made up of white people who would be described as being from the middle-class. It wasn't until I was in the fifth grade that the local, one-room "black school" was closed and the kids from that school began to attend my school.

From this brief account you can see that my formative years were spent in an environment that was anything but diverse. My first real experience with diversity was when I went off to college in the mountains of southeastern Kentucky, where my classmates were largely from the Appalachian regions of Kentucky, Tennessee, and Virginia, as well as from New Jersey and Brooklyn, New York. At Union College in Kentucky, I learned that not everyone else was like the kids with whom I grew up. Especially different were those students from "out East," who were much more sophisticated than me (with my midwestern roots) and my friends from the Appalachian mountain area.

But my college experience with diversity was minimal to what I experienced in my first job as a recreational therapist at Madison State Hospital. Here I was, a middle-class "city boy" (i.e., who had never lived on a farm) interacting with patients who were from farms located in rural southern Indiana. I found out quickly that I knew little about them or their lifestyles.

For instance, I remember in an assessment interview asking a patient what kind of music he liked. He said he liked "string music." By this I thought he enjoyed symphonic orchestra music, while he actually meant he liked country music that featured guitars and banjos. This lack of communication was certainly due to my absence of understanding the patient's cultural background.

Neither was I acquainted with many of the recreation pursuits typically enjoyed by the patients. The most popular card game among the patients was euchre, a game I had never played. The male patients also liked to play washers, a game I had never seen before they taught it to me. And while I had never played pool before working at the hospital, I learned the game to be able to play with the patients, as pool was extremely popular and there was a pool table on every men's ward.

You can see that I had much to learn about the cultural backgrounds of the patients at the hospital. I did eventually come to better understand my clients, but I must admit that I was never completely comfortable with my knowledge of their backgrounds. Of course at the time, the words "cultural diversity" were not yet in our vocabularies, so I just felt "dumb" when it came to understanding the clients I served.

It was a few years later, during the time of my second position as a recreational therapist at Evansville State Hospital, that I first began to truly understand the concept of cultural diversity. This understanding came to me not on the job at my hospital but while attending a recreational therapy conference in Chicago. "Metromorphasis" was the title of the conference. Its focus was on how recreational therapists needed to understand the communities from which their clients came.

We would meet in discussion groups at the Palmer House Hotel in the morning and then go into Chicago neighborhoods in the afternoon. The neighborhood for my group was the Mexican area that contained something like 400,000 people of Mexican decent. I recall our group eating dinner in a small Mexican restaurant where the waitresses only spoke Spanish. This was my first Mexican meal and a cultural awakening for me!

When I returned to Evansville State Hospital I began to see things that had not previously been apparent to me. For instance, many of our patients were from the African American neighborhoods of Evansville. Yet I had never stopped to think how their urban cultural backgrounds might make them different from the majority of our patients who were from small towns of Indiana that were almost exclusively made up of people of German descent. Now I began to see and appreciate the differences in the cultural backgrounds of these patients.

I left my position in Evansville to attend graduate school at the University of Illinois, where again I took unplanned "lessons" on cultural diversity. (Even in the early 1970s I still don't recall anyone actually using the term "cultural diversity.") This time I learned from students with disabilities.

My experiences as a recreational therapist had always been within psych/mental health. I had never had the opportunity to even be around anyone who was a wheelchair user. This quickly changed as many of the students I saw at the Rehab Education Center (where I had an office) were wheelchair users.

As I met the students who used wheelchairs, they impressed me as being extremely bright and very determined to succeed in obtaining a college education. I really admired them. In fact, I held them in such high esteem that you could properly say there was a "halo effect" at work. The students were nearly perfect in my eyes.

One experience forced me to reconsider my stereotyped view of the students who used wheelchairs. That was coaching a wheelchair football team. Here I quickly became aware that the guys were just like any other group of athletes in terms of their personalities. Some were great team players. Others were real "hot dogs" who were out for themselves rather than the team. Most were somewhere in between these two extremes. But none were "perfect."

It was good for me to shatter my unrealistic stereotyped view of the students who used wheelchairs. I came to see these students with disabilities as being very human, just like everyone else. This was another good lesson in a long list of lessons on cultural diversity that I had from my college days through my years as a young professional, and on into my graduate school days.

Today, students in recreational therapy are taught about the concept of cultural diversity. They are instructed about the necessity to develop self-awareness concerning their views of people who differ from them and the importance of gaining knowledge of those clients.

If you are a recreational therapy student reading this, my guess is that you probably don't feel "privileged" to have the opportunity to develop cultural competence through your studies— an opportunity I did not receive as a part of my formal education. Perhaps gaining an understanding of cultural diversity to you is just one more thing to learn.

I can assure you that, as someone who gained his current level of cultural competence "the hard way," that there is merit in the study of cultural diversity. I would urge you to embrace your studies in this important area of professional preparation.

Maintaining Confidentiality

All of us know we shouldn't disclose private information about our clients to anyone outside the clinical team, and even then information should only be shared if it is directly pertinent to a client's case. Certainly others outside the clinical setting should never have access to confidential information.

Yet, perhaps one of the hardest lessons for me to learn as a young recreational therapist was to maintain confidentiality. I was excited about what I was doing and wanted to share my experiences with my friends. And you can imagine that my friends might have been intrigued by stories of what had happened at the local psychiatric hospital and therefore might have encouraged me to tell them about my day at work.

There is a natural tendency for all helping professionals to want to tell others "a good story" related to their work. This tendency is most pronounced among young practitioners who, like I was, are excited about what they are doing in their professional lives and want to share their experiences outside their workplace.

In fact, it is well known that most helping professionals go through a phase in which they find it very difficult to maintain confidentiality. As helping professionals mature they learn (sometimes through bad experiences) that they should not and cannot divulge information about their clients to others.

More mature professionals learn that they must not indulge themselves by revealing confidences to others. If they do, they are being self-centered and putting themselves first before their responsibilities to their clients.

I can recall an instance that occurred in our hospital canteen when I was a young recreational therapist. Thank goodness I wasn't directly involved. What happened was that I observed nursing personnel talking about one of our patients. They even mentioned his name in relating a story about what they considered to be humorous behavior by the patient. Unfortunately for all, family members of the patient were sitting at the next table and overheard the remarks.

Besides being unethical, breaking confidentiality can have negative consequences for the relationship between a therapist and client. Trust can be lost in a minute if the client finds the therapist has broken confidentiality.

Certainly we can all relate to the situation of someone breaking a confidence. Every one of us can recall an instance when a friend betrayed a confidence. When this occurs, trust is lost, and it is hard to maintain that relationship. Similarly our clients will lose faith in us if we break confidentiality.

In the end, confidentiality boils down to each of us being responsible for our own behavior. As helping professionals upon who are clients rely, each of us needs to step up to assume our responsibility to maintain client confidentiality.

Burnout

Burnout occurs when the prolonged mental stress of the job results in a gradual loss of positive feelings about serving as a helping professional. Positive feelings are replaced by negative attitudes and behaviors. Burnout may result in an employee who has blunted emotions, lacks motivation for the job, and quits caring about clients. At its extreme, burnout may even produce feelings of hopelessness, helplessness, and depression.

All helping professionals are susceptible to burnout, but ironically, only good employees burn out. This is because good staff really put themselves into their work. I remember someone once telling me employees who just show up for the check don't burn out, they just rust out. They don't burn out because they never had a fire within them to begin with (Austin, 2009).

Those who burn out typically go through three phases originally identified by Maslach (1982). The first phase is experiencing emotional exhaustion. They simply lack energy for the job. The second phase involves treating clients in a depersonalized fashion and reducing client contact. Finally, in the third phase, those who have burned out experience a greatly reduced sense of accomplishment.

At one time in my career as a recreational therapist, I can recall observing one of my senior colleagues being in the second phase of burnout. This more experienced recreational therapist simply quit going to her programs. Instead she would stay in her office. To cover her trail, she would fabricate the client attendance data we were required to post following every program we conducted.

Why do helping professionals, such as my colleague, burn out? As might be suspected, there are a number of things that can bring about burnout.

In the particular case of my colleague, I think her burnout was at least in part the result of the lack of autonomy often felt by recreational therapists in our department. It often seemed to me that we were kept "under thumb" and not provided autonomous functioning. Accompanying this was often a lack of clarity about what we were permitted to do. The only clarity expressed was when our supervisor let us know we had made a mistake! In general, at that moment in time our department just did not provide a healthy work environment where we recreational therapists could feel we were appreciated and valued.

It has been my personal observation that where there is a strong social support network among the recreational therapists in an organization, that there is much less opportunity for burnout to occur. Feeling social support seems to allow workers to know that others in their work group care about them and what they do. Without social support at work and at home, any helping professional is a possible candidate for burnout due to having little to buffer him or her from the constant stress of the giving nature of any helping profession.

It is too bad that many recreational therapists feel a great deal of guilt when experiencing feelings of burnout. They are good people who don't realize that it is the nature of the work environment that is causing the problem. They internalize the situation, perhaps becoming depressed because they realize they are experiencing a lack of motivation for their job and perhaps emotional exhaustion, a negative attitude toward clients, or a lack of accomplishment.

I can recall a woman approaching me after I had done a workshop session on burnout at a recreational therapy conference. She was so relieved to learn about burnout. Knowing that she was simply encountering burnout (and not a "bad person" as she expressed it) significantly lifted her spirits. I must confess seeing the improvement in her self-view also made me feel good about myself. I was pleased that I had been able to share information about the phenomenon of burnout that was directly helpful to a fellow recreational therapist.

Why Clients Like RT
The Norm of Reciprocity

As I recall, I first encountered the notion of the norm of reciprocity when I was a Ph.D. student at the University of Illinois early in the 1970s. It intrigued me then and still does.

What is the norm of reciprocity? It is an idea from psychology that suggests people possess a tendency to reciprocate by returning the favor when someone does something nice to them or by retaliating when someone does something not so nice to them.

I guess that generally speaking we can say the norm of reciprocity represents a tendency for people to "get even" with others. If someone does something we like, then we feel obligated to return the favor. Of course, the same notion holds when someone does something we do not like, in that we then want to even things up by an unfriendly act toward that person.

But largely, in my mind, I think of the norm of reciprocity as an explanation of the typical reaction people have in returning a positive gesture to another. It is this positive approach that I wish to discuss it in this chapter.

For years, I told students in my university recreational therapy classes that they were privileged because clients tend to like recreational therapists. Because I wasn't exactly sure why recreational therapists were so well liked by their clients, I generally attributed the high degree of liking of recreational therapists to the fact that recreational therapists do things *with* clients, not *to* clients.

Doctors, nurses, and other healthcare specialists typically do things to clients, such as examining them or giving them injections. In contrast, recreational therapists do activities with clients. The therapist-client relationship is more like a "professional friendship" where the recreational therapist is not in a superior position to the client but enters into more of a partnership with the client.

I do believe that the relationships recreational therapists have with their clients are special and help explain why recreational therapists are generally well liked by their clients. But I have also come to the conclusion that there is more to it than I told my students. It is more than doing things with clients, not to them. It is reciprocity that is the key to clients liking recreational therapists.

The idea that reciprocity plays a major role in fostering positive feelings toward recreational therapists came to me as I read a chapter on the topic of reciprocity in Haidt's (2006) book titled *The Happiness Hypothesis.* As I absorbed information about reciprocity in Haidt's book, the thought kept coming into my mind that reciprocity perhaps plays the largest part in fostering the positive relationships recreational therapists enjoy with their clients.

By the way, Haidt well captured the notion of reciprocity by describing it as a "tit-for-tat" (p. 49) reaction where the reactor responds in kind. The "tit-for-tat" experience that I believe bonds clients to recreational therapists in that clients see the recreational therapist as a "nice guy" or "nice gal;" someone who is open, warm, and friendly and typically allows choice and self-direction on the part of clients. Under these circumstances, clients tend to quickly develop an affinity for their recreational therapist or experience a positive "automatic reciprocity reflex," as Haidt (2006, p. 49) would state.

Haidt has provided an everyday example of reciprocity that may help illustrate why recreational therapists develop reciprocated relationship with their clients. His example is that of the salesperson who, to get something from us, gives us something first. A good personal example of this was when I recently received a dollar bill in the mail from a company that asked me to complete a survey. I had been given something (i.e., a $1.00), so I responded to the request to fill out the survey.

Think about yourself. If someone is friendly and helpful to you, what is your natural reaction? My guess (supported by the notion of reciprocity) is for you to positively view the person who was friendly and helpful to you. Further, you would be likely to want to return the favor by doing something for that person.

Now think about how the recreational therapist can use the good will or "social capital" he or she has gained with a client. If the client feels the recreational therapist has done things for him or her, the client will be more likely to reciprocate in terms of trying to do the things the recreational therapist asks of him or her.

Again, think about yourself. If someone you like asks you to do something, are you likely to meet their request? I think you are. Our clients are much like us in their responses. More than once I have seen for myself that, of all the staff, only the recreational therapist could get a client to do something. I would hold that this was because the client/therapist relationship, built on reciprocity, that grew out of gratitude the client felt toward the recreational therapist for what the recreational therapist had done for him or her.

I suspect that the norm of reciprocity is also related to my personal desire to write this book. That is, I am giving back to the profession to repay all those in the profession who have given to me. While I cannot directly return the favor to all of those who have helped me along the way, I can at least indirectly repay my debt to them by sharing what I have learned with the next generation of recreational therapists.

Clinical Supervision

The first time that I heard the expression "clinical supervision" was when a small group of us were consulting at state psychiatric hospitals in Indiana. That must have been sometime in the 1980s.

Ray Benson was the Rehabilitation Director for the Indiana Division of Mental Health. He asked me and a couple of experienced recreational therapists from the state hospital system to accompany him to two state hospitals in order to come up with suggestions to improve treatment programs.

We essentially spent a full day at each hospital. Most of the day was taken up with doing chart audits in which we examined treatment planning and progress notes.

What we found was that while the progress notes could be improved, there was enormous room for improvement in the writing of treatment objectives. Process objectives were mixed with outcome objectives with no differentiation between them. Often times, the treatment objectives lacked specific criteria. In others there were no conditions stated. In short, staff needed a great deal of coaching in writing treatment objectives.

In search of a solution as to how to improve the writing of treatment objectives, we came up with the term "clinical supervision." We suggested that staff with high degrees of proficiency in writing treatment objectives become "clinical supervisors" for those who needed to improve their skills in stating treatment objectives. This type of supervision would be different from the administrative supervision that already existed.

It was only a few months later that I discovered that the term clinical supervision was already in use by kindred professions like psychology and social work. And I found that these professions had been using the term for several years.

The purpose of clinical supervision programs in these professions was twofold. First, clinical supervision was to assist in the development of the staff receiving it. Second, clinical supervision existed to assure a high level of client care through assisting staff to carry out the clinical program as it was intended to be implemented.

I recall writing an article (Austin, 1986) for a recreational therapy journal in which I introduced the notion of clinical supervision programs and suggested that clinical supervision should become an essential element in recreational therapy. About the same time, a student of mine, Bonni Gruver, became interested in the topic of clinical supervision. She and I conducted a survey of university recreational therapy curricula to determine the status of clinical supervision.

What we found was that the vast majority of university faculty believed that university curricula at both the undergraduate and graduate levels should prepare students to give and receive clinical supervision. Yet, our study determined that only about one-half of the universities were providing such preparation (Gruver & Austin, 1990).

A more recent research study (Jones & Anderson, 2004) found that only a small percentage of practicing recreational therapists had received training in clinical supervision as a part of their professional preparation. Based on their findings, the researchers called for all university recreational therapy curricula to include clinical supervision.

From these studies and my personal observations, I have to state that clinical supervision has not received the attention it should from the recreational therapy profession. This situation should not be allowed to exist as the provision of clinical supervision is the major means for staff development.

Note I stated that clinical supervision is needed for staff development. Some may associate the term clinical supervision solely with student interns. Student interns certainly need clinical supervision, but so do all recreational therapists. Even the most senior of recreational therapists can benefit from receiving clinical supervision. Without clinical supervision, the profession of recreational therapy will not thrive as practitioners will not keep growing and developing.

It is my hope that university recreational therapy faculty will make sure their students receive preparation to give and receive clinical supervision. Further, those practitioners who have not received training in clinical supervision should take short courses or attend workshops to assure they gain a working knowledge of clinical supervision.

Those who wish to learn more about clinical supervision may wish to read the chapter titled "Clinical Supervision" in my textbook, *Therapeutic Recreation: Processes and Techniques* (Austin, 2009).

Self-Awareness

As a new faculty member at Indiana University (IU) in the 1970s, it was my task to develop a master's degree program in therapeutic recreation. Anne Binkley was a doctoral student and visiting lecturer at IU at the time. She assisted me in tackling the challenge of designing a new master's degree program that would prepare recreational therapists to serve as clinicians.

With the help of university instructional consultants, it was decided that we should complete a survey of master's prepared recreational therapists in order to identify the competencies needed to be obtained by students completing their master's degrees at IU. The thought was that once the competencies were identified, then we could "package" them into the courses that would make up the master's curriculum.

What do you think was right at the top of the competencies rated by the survey participants? When we examined the results, Anne and I discovered that among the very highest rated competencies was one that read: "To increase and refine self-knowledge" (Austin & Binkley, 1977).

Until the moment we analyzed our results, I had not thought about self-awareness being a primary or core competency needed by master's-prepared recreational therapists. The more I thought about it, however, the more I bought into the notion that as a part of their curriculum our students needed to become aware of just who they were as persons. I came to understand that as a prerequisite to helping others, recreational therapists and all helping professionals must know themselves.

First, recreational therapists must know themselves so that they are reasonably satisfied with themselves before assuming roles as helping professionals. Being dissatisfied with oneself can lead to being too "needy" to truly be giving to others. Being overly concerned about oneself and his or her own needs spells disaster because such an individual is not in a position to put clients' needs before his or her own.

It also makes sense that, because recreational therapists are constantly striving to help others, their clients' needs are primary and have to be given priority over therapists' personal needs. Without a sense of themselves and their personal needs, it would be difficult for recreational therapists to know when their own needs might be getting in the way of meeting their clients' needs.

By the way, emerging helping professionals have a tendency to put themselves first before their clients. This is probably because these young professionals are unsure of themselves and haven't really examined themselves within the context of the dynamics of their interactions with clients. Once they gain more confidence in their abilities and begin to realize the hazards of putting themselves before their clients, they tend to mature and grow beyond their initial tendencies to focus on themselves at the expense of their clients.

Another reason to know oneself is that knowing yourself is helpful to understanding your clients. If you realize, for example, that you can become defensive when you feel under attack, you can better understand defensiveness when it occurs in your clients. Someone once told me that the psychiatric patients that we worked with "were just like us, only more so." I hope you can see that there is a lot of truth in this statement.

Knowing ourselves can be helpful for our more readily gaining insights about our clients. Having a personal experience (e.g., having been defensive) enables us to better understand our clients when they act in a way similar to us. Or said another way, self-knowledge helps us to more easily identify and relate to similar problems experienced by our clients.

Still another reason to know ourselves is to become aware of the values we hold. If we are conscious of our values, we can be careful not to impose our personal values on our clients.

This is not to suggest we should avoid values. It may be a good technique to help clients explore their own values because this may help them to better understand their own behaviors. It may also be appropriate for clients to embrace new values that you have exposed them to. The point is that knowing your own values, you will be conscious of not imposing them on your clients just because you hold them.

Additionally, because we are human, we all possess strengths and weaknesses. Knowing our strengths and limitations allows us to realize when we reach the limits of our competencies so we do not go beyond our abilities to help our clients. Knowing our limitations also permits us work to improve ourselves in areas where we lack competence.

Have I convinced you of the need for self-awareness? If I have, then I hope you will consider making strides to improve your personal level of self-awareness.

Much of what I have written about in this chapter is contained in the section of my book, *Therapeutic Recreation Processes and Techniques* (Austin, 2009), that covers self-awareness. In that portion of my book you will also find suggestions on ways to improve your self-awareness. This information can provide you with a beginning place for your personal self-exploration.

Being a Team Player

I happen to believe that recreational therapists, by their nature, make great team members in any clinical setting. This is because recreational therapists typically work hard to get along with others and to be supportive of others. They also enjoy being on an equal footing with other team members whom they respect and who respect them in return.

Years ago, when I would observe a team when visiting a clinical facility, I could almost always tell which team member was the recreational therapist. That was because the recreational therapist usually remained quiet and left the talking to the doctors, nurses, social workers, and other staff. Happily, this is no longer true.

In recent years, I have observed recreational therapists as active participants in team meetings. Often other team members would turn to recreational therapists for their views. I think this reflects better professional preparation on the part of recreational therapists and a more assertive attitude by those in our profession who see themselves as equals to other professionals.

Generally, interdisciplinary teams come to mind when we think of work teams in clinical settings. The interdisciplinary team or treatment team is made up of those helping professionals who work directly with a group of clients. Other teams, such as management teams, may also be found in health care settings.

No matter the type of team, true work teams are much more than a collection of people who work together. Instead, teams are constituted of members who are accountable to one another, depend on one another, and strive to achieve a common purpose.

In *Therapeutic Recreation Processes and Techniques* (Austin, 2009), I list tips for team members. Let me quickly review some of these here.

The first tip is to be a good communicator. This involves making a point to listen carefully to the views of other team members. It also involves clearly articulating well thought out views.

Another tip is to display respect for other team members and to put trust in them. Good team members know and respect the strengths of others on their team and attempt to draw out these strengths. They also have trust in others on their team and maintain trust through honest communications.

A third tip is to expect some conflict but to strive for consensus. A virtue of having a team is to produce diverse ideas. A diversity of ideas will naturally produce occasional conflicts. Yet team members have to remember the need to produce consensus and to remain united once decisions are made by the team.

Finally, team members need to be team players. Members have to work to maintain the social-emotive functioning of their team by getting others involved, being friendly and supportive of others, and generally being positive.

As I indicated earlier in this lesson, I believe recreational therapists should make great team members. Working closely with others always takes effort, but I think today's recreational therapists should be well prepared to be strong team players.

Being Professional

In the late 1990s, I directed a federally sponsored grant project to produce instructional videos for recreational therapy. This was the Recreation Therapy Video (RTV) Project that was conducted at Indiana University. The videos produced through the project became known as the RTV videos.

One of the RTV videos was titled "Professionalism in Therapeutic Recreation." In this video I interviewed Ann Huston, who was then the executive director of the American Therapeutic Recreation Association (ATRA). As you might expect, in the video we talked about what was meant by professionalism and how recreational therapists exhibit professionalism.

I'm pleased the RTV video series produced a video program on professionalism, because it is a critical topic for students and emerging professionals to consider. I firmly believe that any profession is doomed if its members do not develop strong beliefs in professionalism.

I don't recall exactly how Ann and I defined professionalism, but to me the first thing that comes to mind when I think of professionalism is someone who holds a trusted position that requires expertise (e.g., knowledge and skills) gained as a result of having taken a prescribed course of study.

Professions may also require additional credentials of those who practice in the profession. This is true of recreational therapy. Recreational therapists must hold the minimum of a bachelor's degree in recreational therapy (or therapeutic recreation) and have passed the national certification exam. Additionally, some states require recreational therapists to hold a license in order to practice.

Thus, the first indicator of professionalism in recreational therapy is having obtained a university degree and to have become certified or licensed. Without these credentials, no one should claim to be a professional in recreational therapy. I believe that displaying professionalism, however, goes far beyond this minimum.

To me, a critical indicator of professionalism is being involved in at least one professional association. If a recreational therapist belongs to only one professional association, I believe it should be a national organization, such as the American Therapeutic Recreation Association (ATRA) or the Canadian Therapeutic Recreation Association (CTRA).

There are also state, provincial, and regional professional associations to which recreational therapists can belong. It is my view that membership in these organizations should not take the place of national membership.

State, provincial, and regional organizations do play unique roles that professionals can and should take advantage of. One of those roles is offering opportunities for networking with colleagues who work in clinical facilities that are close at hand. Contacts can be made with those who work in sister agencies. Having built relationships through the professional organization, these contacts can be valuable resources when seeking advice about things like starting a new program, obtaining a resource, or handling a difficult case.

A second role that state, provincial, and regional organizations play is providing a proving ground for emerging professionals. Inexperienced professionals can gain valuable experiences serving within their state, provincial, and regional organizations on committees or as board members. Graining such experiences will provide a needed background as professionals move to leadership roles within national associations.

Of course, state, provincial, or regional professional associations also fulfill the valuable role of advocating for our profession at the state or local level. Those in a state recreational therapy organization, for example, can advocate for a licensure bill with their state legislators. Often such advocacy efforts are supported by a national professional association that has assisted other states with licensure efforts.

Simply holding a membership in a professional organization, of course, is not enough to truly display professionalism. Recreational therapists need to become active within their professional associations. For the young professional, involvement may be simply attending association sponsored workshops and conferences and regularly reading association publications. More seasoned recreational therapists need to assume leadership roles within their professional organizations. Roles such as editing a newsletter or website, serving on an organizing committee for a workshop, holding a board position, authoring an article, or giving a conference presentation are ones that veteran recreational therapists should assume.

In their book on mental health nursing, nurse educators Lynch and Trenoweth (2008) have stated that professionalism is what separates well educated professionals from those who are well intended but who have not learned the clinical skills required to deliver quality care. I like what they have to say and believe view has implications for professionalism in recreational therapy.

These nurse educators have suggested that to be effective clinicians, professionals need to develop self-awareness that includes both public awareness and awareness of necessary professional values. Specifically, they propose that professionals are able to monitor their behaviors and realize how they are seen by the clients with whom they interact in order to offer supportive, compassionate care. True professionals also develop and subscribe to a set of professional values that include being tolerant of clients and realizing the importance of interacting with clients in acceptable ways in times of conflict. Such awareness allows professionals to continually direct themselves toward meeting client needs, not their own needs. In short, true professionals learn to put their clients before themselves.

Closely related to being aware of professional values is having a specific theoretical perspective. True professionals have a conceptual model for practice that they subscribe to. I am very pleased that many recreational therapists have adopted my Health Protection/ Health Promotion Model as the basis of their theoretical beliefs. But whether it is my conceptual model or another, it is critical that professionals have a model on which their practice rests. Without such a model I don't believe RTs can be reflective practitioners.

I strongly believe another behavioral characteristic of professionalism is engaging in continuing and advanced professional development. It has been said that if we don't grow, we will stagnate and eventually die (or at least our lives as ethical, contributing professionals will end). There is some truth in this. We all need to continually expand ourselves. By this I mean, at a minimum, remaining current with practice trends in our profession by attending conferences and workshops and by systematically reading newsletters and scholarly journals.

When I was a young professional, hospital journal clubs were popular avenues for staff to stay up to date. Members of the club would meet once or twice a month to discuss a specific article. It is my impression that such clubs are not as plentiful today, but this is a shame, because they offered a regular means for continuing professional development. Today, there are a number of websites and electronic publications that have information of interest to professionals in recreational therapy. These can prove helpful in the professional development of modern professionals.

At some point, those who wish to remain in the profession may wish to advance their level of practice by becoming master clinicians. Typically this involves graduate-level preparation, usually resulting in a master's degree. I would go so far as to state that if our profession does not encourage advanced preparation for more sophisticated practice that the entire profession runs the risk of not developing or moving forward.

Equally important is that some clinicians return to school to complete their PhDs. Without strong university faculty, who will provide quality instruction for students? Who will do research? Who will author scholarly articles and textbooks to build our body of knowledge?

There are, of course, other indicators of professionalism in addition to those I have focused upon. However, I sincerely believe that once recreational therapy professionals obtain their basic credentials (i.e., degree and certification or licensure), movement toward a high level of professionalism will be assured if they become fully engaged in their professional associations and if they actively pursue continuing and advanced professional development.

Being an Advocate for Our Profession

In my heart of hearts, I know it is good to stretch myself by trying new things. Even so, at times I'm fearful of jumping into something I know little about.

This was certainly true when I initially participated in the American Therapeutic Recreation Association's "Day on the Hill" during ATRA's Midyear Forum held in Washington, D.C. We ATRA members were given tips on how to interact with senators, representatives, or their staffers in sessions the day prior to visiting on Capital Hill. The day of our visit, about 100 of us left the conference hotel in mass to ride the Metro to Capital Hill.

Even though I had received training on what to do, I can recall being nervous as we marched toward our assignments. I had never visited an office of a senator or representative, and the prospect of doing that made me anxious, I must admit.

One thing that eased the situation was that we were put into pairs. My ATRA partner was an extremely attractive recreational therapist in her late 20s. When I tell you this woman was attractive, I mean it in every way. She was very good looking, she was dressed in a flattering suit with a skirt, and she was charming in her social interactions.

Our first appointment was scheduled with the congressman from my home district in Indiana. When we arrived, he was standing in his outer office talking with two men who were promoting the importance of grain sales. I waited. When the congressman was concluding his conversation with the men, I approached him and introduced myself.

Immediately the congressman said he was sorry but he could not talk with me at that moment due to a scheduled vote on the House floor. About then he spotted my highly attractive colleague. He introduced himself to her and all of a sudden his vote did not seem to be so important. He sat down next to Patty and began talking with her. I pulled over a chair so that I could join in the conversation, but it was apparent that the congressman was not all that interested in what I had to say when he could talk with my colleague.

The other stops Patty and I made to the offices of senators and representatives had more of a professional tone to them. We largely met with staffers who cordially received us and typically sat with us around a conference table in the senator's or representative's office.

That evening, back at the hotel, we met with other ATRA members who, like us, had advocated for recreational therapy on Capitol Hill that day. All agreed that it had been an empowering experience to meet in the offices of those we had elected to office to talk about our profession of recreational therapy and our needs in the areas of public policy and legislation.

This was my first real encounter into advocacy, and it had gone well. I felt that I had done a good thing by acting on behalf of our profession, and I took some pride in having been a spokesperson for recreational therapy with those who made public policy for the United States.

I would go so far as to say that I actually liked advocating for our profession. This was a big change for me, someone who initially had great misgivings about even participating in ATRA's "Day on the Hill."

Since that initial experience, I have advocated in Washington, D.C., for our profession several times. Although I didn't have Patty to gain the attention of those with whom I was speaking, I was accompanied by one or more recreational therapy professionals and this "buddy system" always worked well. It seemed that when I didn't know what to say my colleague did. And without fail we thought our professional advocacy accomplished as much as we could have hoped for.

I have come to believe that advocating for our profession is a responsibility that all recreational therapists should assume. If we don't speak out for our profession, who will? In the end, by advocating for our profession, we are advocating for our clients as we push for public policies and legislation that will lead to more and better recreational therapy services being available for our clients.

Learning by Doing

I've always thought of recreational therapy as being a psychoeducational enterprise, because our clients learn new ways of feeling, thinking, or behaving as a result of their direct participation in recreational therapy activities.

I believe this is true not for just mental health but for the entire field of recreational therapy. For example, even in physical rehabilitation, clients are learning to adjust socially and psychologically to their disabilities, as well as learning to regain physical abilities or learning how to adapt to their activity limitations.

As a psychoeducational enterprise recreational therapy provides direct opportunities for learning. Recreational therapy clients achieve new emotions, cognitions, or behaviors through their experiences in activities. Our clients are active learners. They learn by doing.

College students are required to memorize a great deal of information. But all college students know rote memorization is not nearly as effective as experiential learning. We retain knowledge much better when we take it in and deal with it in some personal way. This is what we do in recreational therapy as clients learn through direct experiences.

If the active learning process is facilitated through group-processing techniques (e.g., debriefing) by a skilled group leader, experiential learning can be enhanced. Recreational therapists regularly employ group-processing techniques in order to facilitate their clients' learning processes.

My guess is that you, as recreational therapy students, regularly engage in classroom exercises lead by your instructor that closely resemble recreational therapy group sessions conducted for clients in the field. For instance, you role play therapist/client interactions, and then following your reactions as the role players, you are provided feedback by other students and your instructor.

Borrowing from his or her days in the field, your instructor may even employ a recreational therapy debriefing technique in class. I know that I've regularly used the "What? So What? Now What?" debriefing technique in my RT classes. I've found this approach to be extremely effective in promoting the learning of my students.

Yes, all of us (including our clients) learn best through direct experiences. Recreational therapy provides a wonderful means for clients to learn new ways of feeling, thinking, or behaving within a warm, supportive atmosphere.

It's Good to Give Feedback

Some years ago, Charlie Bullock, John Lewko, and I observed staff interacting with campers with disabilities at a summer camp located at Bradford Woods. If you are not acquainted with Bradford Woods, it is an internationally known outdoor recreation and education center run by Indiana University. The results of our study were published in the therapeutic recreation literature in 1980 (Bullock, Austin, & Lewko, 1980).

What we discovered in our study surprised each of us. We found that staff provided no feedback at all in 20% of the instances when the campers were successful in performing a task in a recreational activity. The campers received not even a pat on the back or a "way to go" or a "nice going" in one out of every five times they did something well.

Perhaps more disturbing was what we observed when campers were not able to succeed. In 16% of the cases in which the campers did not succeed, there was no feedback at all given by staff. This was too bad, because these campers with disabilities needed feedback to both help them to correct mistakes they were making and to receive encouragement from staff so that they would not become discouraged and give up.

As we later reported in our article, all of us (including campers with disabilities) need to be provided feedback for a variety of reasons. One is that if we are not told we are doing well, we may assume that we have failed. For those whose self-esteem might not be high to begin with, a lack of feedback from others might easily be interpreted as a negative assessment of them.

If we are not succeeding at doing something, we can also benefit from getting feedback that will help us to correct errors we are making. We can gain information from the feedback of others that will help us to do better. For instance, feedback such as "just put a little more air under it" may help a basketball player to put more arch his or her shot.

Equally important can be feedback in the form of encouragement. We need to receive motivational feedback in order to persist when learning something – especially when things are not going well. Positive feedback in such an instance might be: "Keep trying. I know you can do it."

I should mention that in our study we found that the staff (most of whom were college students who worked at the camp as a summer experience) did not appear to be aware of their feedback patterns or the possible effects their feedback might have on the children. Because of this, camp administrators soon began to train staff on the necessity to provide proper feedback to campers.

But the need for the proper provision of feedback certainly transcends camping programs for children with disabilities. All recreational therapists need to become aware of the possible effects of feedback on their clients and to learn to deliver positive feedback to their clients.

There are some tips derived from our research that recreational therapists should keep in mind when providing feedback to their clients. One tip is to regularly give feedback to clients who succeed as "no news is bad news" for many clients. If they don't hear positive feedback, they may not realize they are doing well.

Another tip when clients succeed is to give feedback that relates directly to what the client just did. Here an example might be: "I liked the way you put more arch on that shot. Way to go!" This feedback has the added advantage that it is positive and motivational. It is important to keep feedback upbeat so that clients feel supported and encouraged by the therapist's comments.

A final piece of advice is to make statements that pertain to the individual's internal traits when they do well. For instance, the therapist might say: "I really like the way you stuck to trying to do it right. You sure have perseverance!"

When clients don't do well the therapist should say something like: "You just had some bad luck there." Thus, the lack of success is not attributed to a stable trait within the person but to just being unlucky. Of course, we learned earlier that it would be helpful in this instance if the therapist would also give some corrective feedback so the client might be instructed to do better the next time.

In *Therapeutic Recreation: Processes and Techniques* (Austin, 2009), I have listed some additional guidelines for giving feedback to clients in therapy groups. These guidelines originally appeared in Posthuma's (2002) excellent counseling book. Below I have highlighted these guidelines for feedback in the hope that recreational therapists and recreational therapy students may take from them when working with therapy groups.

The first guideline is to be selective in what you say. Don't give information until members of the group are ready to use it. You may have valid observations, but save them for yourself if the group is not ready to gain from them. Also, be selective in giving praise to the group. Overdoing your praise may set up a situation where your praise is not taken seriously or members of the group may feel let down if they think they have achieved all they can.

Another is not to give too much information at one time. Receiving too much information all at once can be overwhelming for group members.

Still another is not to be judgmental in giving feedback. Don't judge members of the group or scold them. Instead, describe what they are doing without being judgmental. Closely related to not being judgmental is to generally avoid confronting members when giving feedback. Before confronting members, the therapist should be sure he or she has established rapport with clients because otherwise group members may become defensive and may be inhibited from freely taking part if they don't feel comfortable in being confronted.

A basic piece of advice in giving feedback is also provided on Posthuma's list. That is to give feedback immediately. Don't wait until the moment has passed to give feedback, but give it when the behavior occurs.

A final tip on giving feedback is to remember that the therapist is a role model for giving and receiving feedback. Group members often learn social behaviors from watching the therapist and how he or she does things. For instance, if you are positive with your feedback, members will likely follow your example. Also, group members will observe you to see how you take feedback from others without becoming defensive.

I hope you can see from this lesson that giving feedback is indeed good. And, further, the type of feedback you give is also important. I know this is very true from my personal experience as a university instructor. The same ideas that therapists apply in working with their groups are ones that I have been able to use with my students in the classroom.

When Clients Change

I have witnessed with my own eyes some remarkable transformations in persons with mental health problems. Perhaps the most startling for me was the case of a middle-aged man I shall refer to as Andrew (not his real name). Andrew was a regular participant in several of our recreational therapy groups at the state hospital where I worked as a recreational therapist.

It is difficult for me to remember all the groups that Andrew took part in. I can recall that Andrew was in my Men's Physical Activity Class, that met three days each week, and he was a teammate of mine on the patient/employee softball team that played in a local church league. (The state hospital team was permitted to play in the church league through the good graces of the local churches since our team represented no church, just the state hospital.)

In addition to being a "regular" in our recreational therapy programs, Andrew was the most paranoid person that I ever encountered. I have often referred to him as "the most paranoid man in the world." It is hard to imagine anyone being more paranoid than Andrew.

Let me illustrate. At one time, Dr. Kelley, the head of the Psychology Department, had a heart attack in his office on the grounds of the state hospital. There was great commotion as the ambulance arrived to take Dr. Kelley to a local hospital. All the state hospital staff liked and admired Dr. Kelley, so to all of our great joy, Dr. Kelley survived and continued to ably serve our patients for many years after.

Prior to Dr. Kelley experiencing his heart attack, Andrew had stopped by Dr. Kelley's office daily to pick up the morning newspaper after Dr. Kelley had read it. Of course, while Dr. Kelley was at the local hospital being treated for his heart condition, the paper was no longer delivered to his office. Andrew actually believed that Dr. Kelley had staged the heart attack so he would no longer have to share his newspaper with Andrew! Now that is paranoid.

There is much more however to the story of Andrew. Years later, I happened to run into Andrew at a local restaurant. By then I had completed my Ph.D. and had become a professor. Andrew had been released from the state hospital and had been working for some time as a custodian for a local bank.

I was at the restaurant where Andrew and I came upon each other with another recreational therapist, Jerry, who also had worked with Andrew years prior at the state hospital. Andrew saw me and Jerry and came over to us. We really didn't know what to expect from him.

We were both delighted to learn from Andrew that he was doing well and had been successfully employed in the community for several years. Then Andrew told us "I want to thank you 'young guys' for helping me so much when I was at the state hospital. You really did a lot for me." (Jerry and I later talked about being termed "young guys" because years had passed, and we no longer would have expected to be called that. We were, however, very young when we worked with Andrew.)

Jerry and I could not believe our ears. Here was the most paranoid man in the world acting very appropriately and thanking us for all that we had done for him. We were amazed, to say the least.

Andrew went on to tell us that after years as a psychiatric patient that he had come to the conclusion that he didn't want to spend the rest of his life at the state hospital. This, he stated, had motivated him to work toward being released into the community and that without the help of the recreational therapists and other supportive staff at the state hospital he would not have been able to leave.

I often told my recreational therapy students the story of Andrew. My students always found it a heartening story because it showed that anyone (even "the most paranoid man in the world!") could change.

We sometimes hear from professionals (including recreational therapists) that they do not have the responsibility to motivate clients to change because it is the responsibility of the clients to want to change. This is too bad, because all clients are capable of change, and client motivation can be changed by means of interpersonal interactions. As Miller and Rollnick (1991) aptly stated:

> As a therapist, you are not a passive observer of your client's motivational states. You are an important determinant of your clients' motivation. "Lack of motivation" is a challenge for your therapeutic skills, not a fault for which to blame your clients. (p.35)

It is probably true that clients will continue to think and behave as they have in the past until some intervention interrupts what has come to be normal for them. At times, change may be motivated by individuals finally "hitting bottom," something they have never experienced. Hitting bottom interrupts what is normal for them and "wakes them up" that they must make a change.

Most of the time, however, change is not so dramatic. People don't "hit bottom," but they progress through a series of motivational stages that move them toward change. Therapists who understand the stages people go through in making changes can do the right things to prompt clients to move toward change.

I have found a wonderful explanation of the dynamics that occur as we motivate clients toward change. It is Prochaska and DiClemente's (1982) Transtheoretical Model. This model details the stages clients go through in making changes.

Perhaps the best way to explain the model is to go over the stages that clients experience as they undergo change. The first is the precontemplation stage. During this stage, clients aren't yet thinking about changing.

With precontemplators, it is usually best not to be confrontive with clients, because they are likely to just become defensive. Neither do they want to be "lectured" or told what is best for them.

There are actually different types of precontemplators, each requiring a different approach. Reluctant precontemplators do not have the knowledge that would motivate change. So providing them with empathetic feedback is a good approach. Rebellious precontemplators don't want others to make decisions for them, so offering them several choices is a good strategy. Resigned precontemplators are overwhelmed by what has happened to them and have lost hope. For them it is important to help them restore hope. Finally, rationalizing precontemplators are clients who have all the answers. They can give you every reason in the world as to why their problem is really not a problem for them. Here the therapist's strategy is to use reflective listening while expressing empathy for the rationalizing client.

The contemplation stage is the second stage. It is reached when clients acknowledge their problem or concern and begin to consider changing. Typical of this stage is ambivalence. Clients are deciding if they want to commit to changing.

Here the appropriate strategy is for recreational therapists to instill hope that change is possible. Therapists try to provide reasons to change, including the risks of not changing. Therapists also attempt to heighten the client's feelings of self-efficacy (i.e., a "can-do" feeling).

The stage following contemplation is the preparation stage. In this phase, clients are committed to change and are planning what they will do in the near future to bring change about.

During the preparation stage, clients are apt to need guidance with their planning in the form of suggesting options they may take, with emphasis on options that have worked for others in the past. Therapists should also talk with clients about possible barriers that may be encountered and potential strategies to deal with anticipated barriers. Therapists may additionally help clients develop coping skills in case things don't go as planned. Finally, clients should be helped to examine their plans of action so they can work out as many details as possible in an effort to avoid their plans being derailed.

After clients have prepared their plans, they enter the action stage. In the action phase, clients actually implement their plans to tackle their problems or concerns. At this time, therapists confirm the clients' plans, monitor clients' activities, support clients in their efforts, and work to increase the self-efficacy levels of clients. In short, therapists attempt to instill an "I-can" attitude.

The maintenance stage is the final stage for successful change. During this phase, clients may continue to need support and encouragement. They may also need skills training to help them to establish new behaviors as old ones are given up. The major role of therapists during this maintenance stage is that of helping clients to prevent relapse.

Of course, there is always the danger of relapse. Relapse may occur during both the action and maintenance stages. The main role of therapists when relapse occurs is to prevent clients from becoming demoralized and to help clients to renew their journey through the processes of contemplation, preparation, and action. Here strategies include providing clients with empathetic understanding about relapse, helping clients identify reasons for the relapse, and reminding clients that time is always needed for stable change to take place.

Thus, Prochaska and DiClemente's stage model can be used by recreational therapists as a basis for motivational strategies. Once the client's stage has been identified the therapist can employ appropriate strategies to help the client progress (Austin, 2009).

I wish I knew the details of how Andrew progressed through the stages outlined. My guess is that he was assisted by therapists, including recreational therapists, who intervened with the strategies suggested by Prochaska and DiClemente. From what Andrew told me and Jerry, he certainly felt he was supported by staff in his efforts to leave the hospital.

When do clients change? Clients change when something or someone intervenes to interrupt their habitual way of thinking or behaving. It is the responsibility of recreational therapists to understand the processes through which clients change so they can intervene with strategies that are appropriate for motivating change in clients.

Engage Your Clients

I believe that perhaps better than other therapy, recreational therapy has the ability to engage clients. The reason is simple. Clients like to take part in recreational therapy because our programs typically allow them to do things they enjoy in a warm, supportive atmosphere.

The reasons clients participate in programs that they enjoy within positive atmospheres has everything to do with the approach taken by recreational therapists. Recreational therapists structure their programs in such a way as to optimize the engagement of clients.

First, it is the nature of recreational therapists to present themselves to clients in a friendly, nonthreatening way. Recreational therapists do things with clients, not to clients. The therapist/client relationship that is one in which the recreational therapist does not indicate he or she is superior to the client, but enters into a kind of partnership where the two work together toward achievement of the clients' goals.

Second, recreational therapists assess clients to find out what clients like to do and what strengths and abilities they possess. Recreational therapists also assess clients' needs. Knowing the clients' needs, strengths, and preferences, recreational therapists can suggest activities to clients that are apt to be helpful to them.

Recreational therapists involve clients in their own planning so that they have a say in determining in which programs they will take part. Thus, clients' preferences are honored within recreational therapy. It is human nature to want to complete those things we humans choose for ourselves so our clients are likely to have positive feelings toward the programs they have selected and be motivated to participate in them.

Third, recreational therapists strive to produce environments where clients are challenged within a supportive atmosphere. Recreational therapists seek to have their clients participate in activities that stretch them but not to the point of breaking. They want clients to feel challenged but not overwhelmed. Of course, it takes some amount of clinical judgment on the part of recreational therapists to put their clients in the right situations that will provide opportunities for mastery with minimal frustration. But whatever the situation, recreational therapists are ready to offer corrective feedback and psychological support to clients when they don't succeed.

Aggression Begets Aggression

In their recreational therapy courses, my students had studied aggression and knew the fallacy of thinking that people can reduce aggression by being aggressive. Unfortunately, the educations of some of the psychiatrists they worked with were less complete.

I can't tell you how many times my former students have reported to me that a psychiatrist at the hospital where they worked ordered that a heavy bag be installed so that patients might punch it to get rid of their aggression. This is sad, because any psychiatrist who had heavy bags installed was simply following old notions derived from Freudian psychology and was out of touch with the modern research evidence on aggression. Let me explain.

Freud's theory held that aggression was a basic drive. So according to Freudian theory, aggression had to continually be released or it would build up to the point that the person would "explode" with a tremendous release of the aggression that had built up. The concept has also been described as producing a hydraulic effect where aggression, like water behind a dam, must be let out or it will build up to the point that it would burst.

This concept that aggression could be reduced by releasing aggression has been termed the "cathartic notion." This expression catharsis comes from the Latin word "catharticus" that means to purge. Thus, those who subscribe to the cathartic notion believe people can purge aggression by being aggressive.

When I was a young recreational therapist in the 1960s, we subscribed a Freudian view of aggression. We thought that if we allowed our psychiatric patients to engage in aggressive recreational activities, they could reduce their aggressive behaviors. We had patients hit a punching bag (the small bag filled with air) and a heavy bag (the long, big stuffed bag). We even had our patients bowl with the thought that they could purge their aggression by knocking down the bowling pins.

Modern research has, however, not been kind to the cathartic notion. In fact, one social learning research study after another has shown that allowing people to be aggressive just brings on more aggression, not less. (See Austin, 2009, for a discussion of available research.). As social psychologists are fond of stating, aggression begets aggression.

Due to the lack of evidence to support it, the cathartic notion would not be followed by enlightened mental health professionals. Recreational therapists would no longer engage clients in aggressive activities to rid them of aggression.

So what should today's recreational therapists do to help their clients reduce aggression? What recreational therapists do is to find ways in which clients can reduce the tension that accompanies aggression without being aggressive.

When helping clients to select tension-reducing activities, it is important that they avoid those that may produce further frustration, such as competitive sports where losing may be frustrating. Examples of activities that have tension reducing properties but are nonaggressive and noncompetitive are jogging and swimming.

So the next time you hear an unenlightened individual claim that clients should engage in aggressive activities in order to reduce aggression, you will be able to tell them that research has not supported the cathartic notion. Further, you can suggest that the best activities for aggressive clients are those that have tension-reducing properties and are not competitive or aggressive.

Use Self-Disclosure Sparingly and in a Timely Way

Self-disclosure is a therapeutic technique that may be employed effectively by recreational therapists. The intent of self-disclosure is for the therapist to personally disclose an experience that he or she has encountered if it relates to a similar situation, thought, or feeling experienced by the client. Self-disclosure may also be used to disclose to the client personal feelings that the therapist is experiencing as he or she interacts with the client.

There are some rules that apply to the use of self-disclosure with clients. One is that self-disclosure should not be used early in the therapist-client relationship. The recreational therapist should develop rapport with any client prior to self-disclosing.

I guess a general rule that applies to all parts of the therapist-client relationship is that "it is about the client, not us." By this, of course, I mean that the focus is always on the client and what is best for him or her. Recreational therapists should never tell stories about their pasts to build themselves up for their own ego gratification. Instead, they should relate their own experiences only when they believe that relating their personal experience will be therapeutic for the client.

I have thus far been discussing self-disclosure as a technique whereby the recreational therapist tells a single client his or her past experiences or discloses how he or she is reacting to a situation. Many times, however, recreational therapists are not working in one-on-one situations but are working with groups.

Can self-disclosure be used in group leadership? Yes, it can be, but as with individuals it needs to be carefully applied.

One of the authors on group counseling that I have very much enjoyed reading is Professor Gerald Corey. Corey (1995) has suggested that as a technique with groups, self-disclosure should be employed to provoke feelings of encouragement, acceptance, and support within the group. He does, however, suggest that a group leader may occasionally employ self-disclosure to disclose how he or she is affected by the group's lack of participation.

Based on my personal experience, I think Corey's suggestion of using self-disclosure with a group that is lacking participation is an excellent one. When I was a young professor at the University of North Texas, I told my students an "urban legend" to illustrate how a person's behavior could be affected by social reinforcement. The urban legend was that students in a class at the University of Illinois (where I had done my Ph.D.) only would attend to the professor when he moved to his right. By the end of the class session the students had the poor professor lecturing while crowded into the far right corner of the classroom!

The next class session, after relating this urban legend to my North Texas students, I entered the classroom and began to give my lecture for the day. A couple of students were reading the newspaper. Others were looking out the windows at what was a beautiful sunny day. A couple more seemed to be sleeping. Still others in the back of the room were talking together. No one was paying any attention to me!

Not knowing how to respond to the inattentiveness of my students, at first I just spoke faster and louder. But to no avail. They still didn't listen.

So I did something that I had never done in my life. I pushed away the podium on which my class notes were placed and stepped forward toward the students. I disclosed to the students: "I don't know what is going on here but no one is paying any attention to my lecture and I am angry about it!"

The class broke into laughter. Before I had arrived in the classroom they had decided to reinforce me by being attentive only if I moved to my right (which I never did because I just stayed at the podium grabbing it tighter and tighter as I became more and more frustrated in my attempts to get the attention of my inattentive students). The students were trying out the reinforcement theory we had discussed in class the session before.

It turned out that both the students and I learned from this experience. They learned that you have to get the person to behave as you wish them to before they can be reinforced (which can be difficult). I learned that self-disclosure was a technique that I could, and did later, successfully employ with other students.

Of course, as Corey (1995) has warned, it would be a mistake to think "the more disclosure, the better," as self-disclosure should be used sparingly. Corey has also reminded us that it is not appropriate "to let it all hang out" without really considering the reasons for using self-disclosure, the readiness of the group for it, the potential impact your story may have on them, and the degree that your story is relevant to the group at that moment in time.

So the question is not should self-disclosure be used by recreational therapists. It is how much and when it is appropriate to employ self-disclosure.

Be Supportive of Clients

All of us want to receive emotional support from others. We particularly like to receive supportive statements from those whose opinions we value the most. This is human nature. Thus, recreational therapists need to make a conscious effort to be supportive in their interactions with their clients.

This doesn't mean recreational therapists should give hollow compliments to their clients. But it does mean that recreational therapists should not miss opportunities to provide clients with supportive statements and they should never make negative statements about clients.

Supportive statements may be simple ones such as complimenting a client on his or her appearance. "I like your new shirt," you might say, "it is really good looking." Such a comment might be particularly appropriate if made to a client who was shy and unsure of how he presented himself or herself.

There are a great number of opportunities in recreational therapy to compliment clients. Think for a minute about what typically occurs within recreational therapy programs. If you do, I believe you will quickly arrive at a conclusion. That conclusion is that because clients are constantly behaving in activities, there are many chances for their behavior to be commented upon.

For instance, recreational therapists may compliment clients on the ways they take part in activities. "I really liked the way you shared your crayons with Billy today. You are good at sharing," a recreational therapist might tell a child. Or if a client makes a real stride in his or her treatment, the recreational therapist can recognize this by pointing out the client's success and praising the person for the effort or persistence put into obtaining the therapeutic outcomes.

In making supportive statements, it is critical that recreational therapists attribute positive outcomes directly to the client's abilities or personality traits. Making internal attribution statements places the cause of success with the client. If the client receives supportive comments in the form of praise for what he or she has done, the person will be apt to feel good about his or her performance and to experience enhanced self-esteem.

It certainly is important to make supportive statements to clients that attribute their successes to them. But perhaps it is even more important to avoid attributing negative outcomes directly to the client. A client should never be made to think he or she is "bad" or "a loser" because of a lack of success at doing something. Instead, recreational therapists should make supportive statements that help the client to see negative outcomes as isolated events that are not indicative of the client's personality.

Supportive recreational therapists attempt to attribute negative outcomes to the situation (e.g., "No one could hit a pitch thrown that fast!"), the need to make an adjustment in technique, such as shooting a basketball (e.g., "Just put a little more air under your shot, and I think you'll start hitting it."), the need for more effort (e.g., "I know you can do it if you really focus."), or just plain bad luck (e.g., "You really haven't had any luck today.").

In short, recreational therapy provides many opportunities to make supportive comments to clients. These are opportunities that should not be missed by recreational therapists.

The Use of Gimmicks Can Be Good

Recreational therapy groups are typically made up of six to 12 members and are facilitated by one or two recreational therapists. Promoting interactions among the group members is a key to the success of any recreational therapy group.

Leaders of recreational therapy groups often select exercises or activities to facilitate interaction on the part of members. I like to refer to such exercises or activities as "gimmicks," because they tend to be clever and novel in nature, and they are kinds of tricks that recreational therapists can pull out of their proverbial hats when they wish to achieve certain ends with groups. (I realize that some would not consider such group exercises to be gimmicks but, instead, think of them as tools. Differences in categorizing something as a gimmick should not cloud the points I am making in this chapter.)

Some caution needs to be used when selecting gimmicks to employ with recreational therapy groups. This is because exercises that are not well chosen may be perceived by participants as being demeaning to them or as only trendy time fillers.

But in the case of icebreakers, I have to say that they are generally good gimmicks for leaders to use in getting recreational therapy groups started. Of course, even icebreakers must be appropriate for the group with which they are being used.

The term "icebreakers" comes from the expression of "breaking the ice," meaning people becoming comfortable with a situation by reducing their levels of tension and anxiety. Such tension reduction and comfort enhancement are highly desirable in group work.

In order to build a safe atmosphere in which members feel free to interact, it is important to get any group off to a good start. This is particularly true with members of recreational therapy groups who often feel isolated or apart from others. Such feelings may even lead these group members to believing they are unlikable and are not desirable to be around—leaving them feeling extremely uncomfortable with group participation.

Thus, icebreaking exercises can be ideal activities for recreational therapy groups. This is because icebreakers tend to immediately set a positive tone for the group by involving members in group activities that have the purpose of putting them at ease.

Icebreakers also have the effect of allowing members of a group to get to know one another. By learning about one another, group members begin to become familiar with each another and to discover commonalities that often help them to bond.

Participants also reveal information about themselves to the group leaders during icebreakers. This information may prove helpful to the leader in establishing rapport with individuals or in discovering abilities or personality traits that later can be used as client strengths in planning interventions.

Even though certainly seasoned recreational therapists are knowledgeable about icebreakers, it may be that recreational therapy students have not had extensive experience with icebreakers. So let me describe, as examples, a couple I have regularly used with success over the years with all types of groups varying in age from college age to mature adults.

One icebreaker is called "Peter/Paul." In this exercise group, members get together in dyads (i.e., pairs). Each person interviews the other to find out information to use in introducing his or her partner to the group. Then each individual takes turns introducing the other by standing behind that person and speaking in first person as though they were that individual. The person being introduced has to remain quiet and can only correct erroneous information once the introduction has been completed. This activity produces a great deal of fun and inevitably as much is learned about the person doing the introducing (as he or she reveals themselves through their actions) as the person being introduced.

Another example of an icebreaker that I have had success with is the "best friend" exercise. The leader of this exercise gives out pieces of paper to each group member. On the papers are questions for them to answer as their best friend would respond. Questions might read something like, "My best friend would say the three things I like doing most in my leisure time are…." or "My best friend would say three things other people do that most rub me the wrong way are…." I've found that people are often much more open about themselves when they "let" their best friend describe them.

"Side effects" of using icebreakers are that they often have the effect of loosening people up for further participation in the group as they become energized and motivated through the enjoyment they receive from doing something with members of the group. Participation in icebreakers can also help bond group members by giving them common experiences. Such bonding may provide the group with a sense of feeling they belong as a unit, or you might say they have a feeling of "groupness."

I should also add that I have used warm-up exercises successfully with groups. As with icebreakers, I have used warm-up exercises with a variety of populations of various ages.

Although, like icebreakers, warm-up exercises must be well chosen, they can be used to "get groups going" (i.e., to get group members interacting). Many warm-up exercises can also be used as "first comer" activities for those who arrive early for a group session.

The warm-up exercise that I like most is called "Signatures." In this activity, the group leader makes up a sheet on which appear 20 to 30 items (depending on the size of the group) that describe someone or something or some accomplishment. Items for example might be: "Have been to a Bruce Springsteen concert" or "Have seen the movie *Hoosiers*." or "Am over six feet tall," or "Worked for five years or more in my job." Group members then circulate within the group to collect as many signatures as possible (only being allowed to get one signature from each group member) before the leader tells them the time is up for collecting signatures. After the signatures have been collected, the group leader usually asks participants how many signatures they collected and gives the person with the highest number some reward in the form of a round of applause from the group or some small gift (e.g., candy bar).

In closing this lesson, I want to acknowledge that gimmicks such as icebreakers and warm-up exercises are activities that simply speed up processes that would probably naturally occur within groups without their ever being used. Group members would no doubt eventually become comfortable with each other without icebreakers, but the process might take some amount of time. Group members probably would eventually interact with one another without warm-up exercises but, again, it might take a while for this to happen. Thus icebreakers, warm-up exercises, and similar activities sometimes referred to as "energizers" (to energize groups) or "deinhibitizers" (to help members become less inhibited) provide "short cuts" for group leaders who wish to help their groups develop. If these exercises help groups to better function, then I believe they are good gimmicks.

Employ and Foster Intrinsic Motivation

Intrinsic motivation is essentially doing some self-determined activity because of the love for the activity due to having interest in it, the challenge it offers, or the enjoyment it provides. Intrinsic motivation comes from within the person, not from outside forces such as external rewards or pressures.

In contrast, extrinsic motivation comes from the environment. People are said to engage in extrinsically motivated activities when they do so as a means to an end, such as recognition or money.

For recreational therapists, intrinsic motivation is something they can employ toward the benefit of their clients. Intrinsic motivation is also something recreational therapists attempt to foster in their clients.

Intrinsic motivation may be seen to be a gift for recreational therapists. This is because, by understanding their clients' intrinsic motivation systems, recreational therapists can apply this information for their clients' benefits.

This is accomplished by first assessing their clients to find out what recreation or leisure activities they are intrinsically motivated to do. Once the clients' interests are identified, this information can be used as a basis for helping them to achieve their treatment, rehabilitation, or wellness goals.

Information about clients' recreation and leisure interests is actually applied in two ways. One is for clients to participate in the identified activities in order to receive the positive outcomes they typically receive from their intrinsically motivated participation—outcomes such as experiencing positive emotions, enhancing self-esteem, and increasing self-efficacy.

The other way knowing about clients' recreation and leisure interests can be helpful is for recreational therapists and their clients to identify strengths that allow clients to enjoy their chosen activities. Once identified, these strengths can become resources to help clients to reach their goals.

For instance, intellectual abilities or athletic abilities might be identified strengths that a client might draw upon in overcoming a problem. Personality traits such as determination and perseverance that a client relies upon for successes in recreation or leisure activities may be employed as client resources. Clients often have strengths not initially apparent to them that can be drawn upon once the strengths are realized.

The identification of intrinsically motivated recreation and leisure activities and the recognition of client strengths that allow them to enjoy these activities then form the foundation for the strength-based approach that is a central element in recreational therapy. In fact, this is the essence of the strength-based approach.

Recreational therapists also work with clients to increase their intrinsic motivation for change. They strive to encourage clients to become self-determining to the greatest extent possible. This approach helps clients move toward independence, which is an overriding mission of recreational therapy, and avoids the resistance that can easily follow when decisions are made for clients. Like all of us, clients are most likely to pursue change if they originate goals for themselves and are in accord with interventions to be employed, rather than having them imposed by staff.

Recreational therapists are supportive, not directive. Recreational therapists foster freedom and encourage independent decision making. Support, collaboration, and mutual participation are hallmarks of recreational therapy activities that take place in a warm, accepting, and affirming atmosphere in which clients are free to let their self-actualizing tendencies take hold.

Here and Now

The expression "here and now" relates to the immediate events that occur during recreational therapy. It is the here and now that is largely what recreational therapy is all about—not what happened to clients in the past or fantasies about the future.

In fact, much of recreational therapy seems to have a great deal of similarity with Gestalt Therapy in terms of its emphasis on the here-and-now. Panman and Panman (2006) have written this about Gestalt Therapy: "The focus of Gestalt Therapy is always on what is, on awareness of the present moment, and not what might have been (regrets about the past) or what should be (worry about the future)" (p. 53).

Recreational therapy to a large degree mirrors what Panman and Panman stated about Gestalt Therapy. Within recreational therapy, clients become engaged in direct experiences that help them to become aware of their present (i.e., here and now) behaviors, feelings, and thought processes. This focus is perhaps most pronounced within recreational therapy programs serving clients with problems in mental health.

The basic concept in both recreational therapy and Gestalt Therapy is the provision of experiential learning. Through direct experiences (i.e., not talk but active participation) clients become aware of ways they act, feel, and think.

Within recreational therapy, recreation and leisure activities provide opportunities for experiential learning. These activities serve as microcosms of what tends to happen to clients in their "real lives."

When clients are dysfunctional within recreational therapy sessions, they can become aware of their behaviors, thoughts, and feelings as a first step to change them. For example, a client's interpersonal problems will likely reveal themselves while having to interact with others in recreation or leisure activities. Once the client recognizes problems exist, he or she can begin to take steps to correct a problem area.

If clients are functional during recreational therapy, these behaviors can be immediately acknowledged in the here and now. Recreational therapists and other group members can let a client know when he or she does something well. Such feedback has the potential of not only reinforcing behaviors but increasing self-esteem and self-efficacy because people's self-views are heavily influenced by how significant others evaluate them.

Group processing may be used by recreational therapists as a technique to help assure clients learn from their direct here-and-now experiences in recreation and leisure groups. Following participating in a group activity, group processing may be conducted, at which time members discuss and analyze the dynamics of what went on and then apply what has been learned to the real world.

Group processing, then, is a technique that allows group members to gain self-awareness from their participation in group activities in the here and now. Insights gained from group members' direct participation can be extended beyond the group in which they are revealed to their everyday lives.

Build Self-Esteem

It seems to me that when I first entered recreational therapy practice, that there was much more talk about self-esteem and the importance of self-esteem enhancement than there has been in recent years. If it is a reality that recreational therapists today are not emphasizing the enhancement of self-esteem, I think it is a shame.

Self-esteem should take center stage within recreational therapy. I believe that recreational therapists can and should be a force for bringing about positive change in self-esteem.

If it has become "unfashionable" for recreational therapists to focus on their clients' self-esteem, I definitely believe it is time for a change. I would hope it is evident to most in our profession that our clients' self-views greatly affect how they think and how they behave. I would also hope it is realized by recreational therapists that they have the ability to help clients to alter their self-esteem. Hopefully this lesson will shed some light on the topic of self-esteem.

I should comment that some confuse self-concept and self-esteem. The easiest way to differentiate the two is to think of self-concept as being much more global than self-esteem. Self-concept has to do with all self-knowledge people have about themselves. Self-esteem, on the other hand, deals with the affective part of self. Self-esteem has to do with how people value themselves or how favorable they feel toward themselves. In short, self-esteem is the attitude people hold about themselves.

Self-esteem is important first because it affects people's levels of happiness. If people feel they are persons of worth and have the respect of others, they will believe they deserve happiness. Those who have high self-esteem are also happier, because their positive dispositions seem to buffer them against stressors and help them to remain better adjusted. They even have higher levels of physical health.

In contrast, if people's self-views are that they are not persons of worth and are not respected by others, they are apt to feel they are "bad" and undeserving of experiencing joy and happiness. Such feelings can lead to psychological difficulties and even self-destructive behaviors. Low self-esteem individuals are much more susceptible to anxiety, depression, and maladjusted behaviors such as alcohol and drug abuse and violence and crime (Leary, Tambor, Terdal, & Downs, 1995).

Self-esteem is also important because it affects the way people approach life. Those with high self-esteem tend to think they can cope with life's challenges. They believe they have the capacity to succeed. We might say they enjoy feelings of self-efficacy because they will persistently strive toward their goals knowing they will ultimately have success. On the other hand, the dispositions of those with low self-esteem are such that they lack confidence in their abilities. They are unsure of themselves, avoid challenges, and when they do try something, they tend to give up when they encounter failure.

Unfortunately, our clients in recreational therapy too often experience low self-esteem. They feel "foolish, ashamed, inadequate, or awkward," in contrast to those with high self-esteem who feel "pride, self-satisfaction, and confidence" (Leary, Tambor, Terdal, & Downs, 1995).

The negative feelings experienced by individuals with low self-esteem prevent them from engaging in joyful living and have them lacking the confidence they need to succeed in meeting life's challenges. With this being true, it seems to me that recreational therapists need to acknowledge that self-esteem is frequently a problem for their clients and that it should be a major concern for both them and their clients.

If I have convinced you that recreational therapists need to actively intervene to help their clients to improve their self-esteem, you might be asking yourself: "How can self-esteem be enhanced?" The answer is that self-esteem is largely altered by the verbal and nonverbal messages people receive from others. Our self-esteem is sensitive to others' reactions to us.

So in order to enhance their self-esteem, it is important for clients to gain positive reactions from others. Leary (1999) has explained that "events that raise self-esteem are those that increase a person's perceptions of being accepted and included – achievement, recognition, compliments, admiration, and the like" (p. 210).

Recreational therapists need to help clients to gain positive feedback from others that leads them to feel accepted and included. There are a number of strategies to accomplish this.

One way for clients to receive positive feedback from others is to do the things they are good at. If clients can gain recognition for being good at something, they can develop feelings of confidence in their abilities. So a self-esteem strategy for recreational therapists is to structure situations so clients are able to display their strengths, achieve success, and receive positive feedback from others for those achievements.

On the other side of the coin, recreational therapists must be careful to help clients to avoid negative social comparisons, according to Gergen and Gergen (1986). These social psychologists suggest avoiding putting clients into a group where they will pale in comparison to other group members. I have written elsewhere: "Placing a client in situations where everyone else is clearly superior in some way (e.g., possessing a highly developed recreational skill) can negatively impact self-esteem as clients will not feel they are seen in a positive light (i.e., are not positively evaluated by others) or belong with those who are superior in some way (i.e., are not accepted by others)" (Austin, 2009, p. 404).

Another strategy to raise self-esteem has been proposed by Gergen and Gergen (1986). They base this approach on the human trait that people tend to identify themselves with things they perceive as being distinctive about themselves. So the recreational therapist can help clients to perceive some special positive characteristics in themselves that they were not aware of and use them to gain recognition.

I explained this strategy elsewhere in this way:

> If a client is a particularly good athlete or sharp dresser, the therapist can emphasize these positive characteristics that set the client apart. Clients who have collections as hobbies may be encouraged to make others aware of their interests because their collections represent symbols of their distinctive selves in which they can take pride. By emphatically focusing upon those things that are distinctive about clients, the therapist is providing the

implication to clients that these things are evaluated positively by others and valued by others. (Austin, 2009, p. 404).

Still another strategy proposed by Gergen and Gergen (1986) is that of having clients assume social roles in which they are not comfortable but in which they realistically should enjoy success. I have explained: "For example, if a client is reluctant to join in a recreational group because he or she is shy, encouraging participation by the client may lead to feelings of newfound confidence when the client is able to achieve success within the group and, thus, feel he or she belongs (i.e., achieves social acceptance) (Austin, 2009, p. 404).

A general principle for recreational therapists to keep in mind when helping clients to increase their self-esteem is that feeling accepted and liked enhances self-esteem. Leary, Tambor, Terdal, and Downs (1995) have explained that "people's feelings about themselves are highly sensitive to how they think they are being regarded by other people. The more support and approval people receive, the higher their self-esteem tends to be."

Self-esteem can't be bestowed on clients by recreational therapists. Yet, as I have tried to demonstrate, there are a number of strategies that recreational therapists may employ to help clients to achieve greater self-esteem. All strategies call for clients themselves to gain from the responses of others because self-esteem is something that clients achieve as a result of the positive feedback they receive from others.

Leisure Counseling

One of my greatest disappointments in my career in recreational therapy has been the lack of development in the provision of leisure counseling. In the 1960s, when I was a young recreational therapist, I saw leisure counseling (then termed recreation counseling) as one of the most promising areas for our profession. Yet leisure counseling has never developed as I anticipated it would. Even today, leisure counseling remains perhaps the most underdeveloped area of recreational therapy.

I'm not sure as to why leisure counseling has not developed as I envisioned it would, but I have some hunches. Perhaps recreational therapists have simply lacked knowledge of both the theoretical underpinnings for doing counseling and the counseling skills required to do leisure counseling. Perhaps some in, or related to, our profession just did not believe we should be engaged in the level of clinical practice implied by the term leisure counseling.

This idea that recreational therapists traditionally lacked counseling theory and skills is supported by the fact that much of the leisure counseling done in recreational therapy has been simply matching client interests with leisure resources. For example, if someone likes to bowl, the recreational therapist lets the client know where bowling lanes are located. Or if someone wishes to gain a recreational skill, such as learning to dance, the recreational therapist would help the client to locate instructional programs in the community. A low level of counseling knowledge or skills is required to provide this type of leisure counseling.

Having seen these information-sharing programs in action, I can state that most of the recreational therapists conducting them were proud to be doing what they considered to be leisure counseling. Yet I know that hardly any of these individuals has been trained in counseling. They thought they were doing leisure counseling but, in fact, their programs might better have been described as informational at best.

There were others who avoided even the use of the term leisure counseling, preferring instead to use "leisure education." I believe the conscious avoidance of the expression leisure counseling in favor of the term leisure education was due to the fact that many did not believe recreational therapists should be doing any type of counseling. Many of those promoting the use of the term leisure education felt comfortable with the use of an educational paradigm within recreational therapy but not with the provision of counseling.

Some of those who "pushed" leisure education over leisure counseling also believed that recreational therapy should not be "clinical" (as the term counseling would signify) but should simply offer recreational opportunities for persons who were ill or disabled. They didn't view our profession as one that provided specific therapeutic interventions but one that had the end of engaging clients in recreational activities.

It is a real shame that recreational therapy has not developed leisure counseling to any large extent. To do so today it seems that two areas of competence need to be established. Both can be accomplished by providing training through short courses for practitioners or within university professional preparation programs.

One area of competence needed to develop leisure counseling is to educate practitioners and students on the types of leisure counseling that may be offered to clients and the structures in which these may be provided. There are higher levels of leisure counseling than the previously discussed relatively low level informational model of matching clients' interests with available leisure resources, and there are several structures in which they can be delivered.

For example, recreational therapists can work with clients to help them develop an awareness of their leisure lifestyles. In doing so, clients become aware of their leisure values, patterns, and behaviors, as well as recognizing barriers to full leisure participation.

A related area for leisure counseling is helping clients to deal with leisure-related behavioral problems. This might involve helping clients to explore feelings of boredom or behaviors, such as excessive television viewing, and then assisting them to develop strategies to overcome these problems.

Another area for leisure counseling can be decision making. In this form of leisure counseling, clients can learn to make self-determined choices about their leisure lives. This can be a significant benefit for clients who have exercised little choice making in the past.

Still another area for leisure counseling is helping clients to appreciate leisure. In this type of leisure counseling, clients become aware of leisure as a phenomenon and begin to recognize the physical, psychological, and emotional benefits to be found in leisure. Leisure appreciation can also include assessing clients' leisure attitudes.

Structures for leisure counseling can include group formats such as social skills training groups, community reintegration programs, and leisure counseling groups. Individual leisure counseling can also be offered by recreational therapists.

The second area of competence to develop leisure counseling is for recreational therapists to receive training in the dynamics of leisure counseling. Here the concern is with learning about theoretical models for leisure counseling and about the counseling skills necessary to deliver leisure counseling.

Although not extensive, there is literature on theoretical leisure counseling models. I have introduced these theoretical perspectives in the section on leisure counseling in my book (see Austin, 2009). Interestingly, as mentioned in my book, much of today's literature on leisure counseling appears in British journals.

In terms of counseling skills, these should be second nature for recreational therapists, as the professional preparation of recreational therapists should include skills in therapeutic communication that can easily be applied in leisure counseling. For more information on therapeutic communication skills, see my book, *Therapeutic Recreation: Processes and Techniques* (Austin, 2009) for the chapter on that topic.

It is my strong desire to see leisure counseling gain a prominent place within recreational therapy. There is no reason in my mind why leisure counseling cannot flourish within recreational therapy if today's recreational therapy students and practitioners wish to take command of this important area for practice.

Activities Spur Conversation

Recreational therapy is not a talk therapy. It is action oriented. Yet there are times when recreational therapists wish to stimulate conversation with clients.

An example of a time when it is important to have a conversation with a client would be when completing an initial assessment. In this instance, the recreational therapist is attempting to learn about the client and the client's concerns.

Sometimes it is difficult for clients to talk about themselves in order to report information that might prove helpful to the assessment. Many clients, for example, do not have high verbal skills that allow them to reveal information about themselves.

A "trick" I learned early on in my career in order to facilitate conversations with clients was to involve them in some recreation activity. Once they were focused on the activity, I could ask questions of them and observe their level of engagement (e.g., really got involved in the game) and interaction patterns (e.g., rarely maintained eye contact with me).

I often played checkers or worked a puzzle with the client. Sometimes the client and I would shoot pool.

When focusing on the activity, the conversation with me seemed to become secondary to the activity. Clients seemed to be much less conscious of themselves. They would talk freely with me, much as they might when taking part in a recreation activity with a friend.

We recreational therapists were not the only ones who used activities as vehicles to stimulate conversations with clients. I can recall young social workers coming into the hospital recreational therapy office to get the key to the gym so they could take a teenager to the basketball court to shoot baskets as they talked with the youth.

Use Touch Therapeutically

There are instances where words just cannot express our feelings. At these times, touch offers a basic means of nonverbal communication to help us display our emotions. Touch in fact is often portrayed as the most fundamental of all senses.

Yet some helping professionals will not use touch with clients. Years ago I believe many professionals avoided the use of touch with clients due to our Puritan heritage that frowned on touch. I don't know that Puritanism any longer negates the use of touch. Today it is more likely that professionals avoid touch to protect themselves from legal or ethical charges.

It's too bad that some professionals will not touch clients. The therapeutic value of touch has been known for some time. We often have heard phrases such as "a calming touch" or "a healing touch." Scientific evidence has supported the therapeutic benefits of touch in both medical and psychiatric settings (see Austin, 2009).

A colleague once indicated to me that he would never employ touch with clients for fear that a client might misinterpret his action and charge him with unethical behavior. To me this is too bad.

I take the opposite position. I believe we should use touch therapeutically. We can use touch to let clients know that we care about them. Warm, caring touch can do much to boost the motivation or enhance the moods of our clients. A hand on the shoulder, pat on the back, a handshake, or a hug can mean a lot to a client.

Of course, we should employ commonsense when using touch. It is important to consider the setting and the history of the client when using touch therapeutically. For example, I would not hug a client if I were alone with that client. Also, I would avoid using touch with a client that had been sexually abused or had been sexually promiscuous.

The therapeutic use of touch by any professional is a personal decision. But I hope you will not be a recreational therapist who withholds touch from your clients. If you are comfortable with touch, my advice is for you to use it as a therapeutic tool.

Therapeutic Communication Skills Are Not Esoteric

Just what skills are involved in therapeutic communication? A long list of skills needed for therapeutic communication can be constructed.

In fact, I've listed a number of questions in the list that follows that may offer a sense of the skills involved in therapeutic communication. See how many you can answer.

- Are you familiar with how the speaker's attitude toward the client affects communication?
- Can you explain how the use of vocabulary and voice clarity, tone, and volume affect communication?
- Do you understand listening from the perspective of a client? Are you aware of potential external barriers to listening?
- Do you know that most people lack the skills to be effective listeners?
- Can you identify the four primary means to attentive listening?
- Do you know how to employ paraphrasing, clarifying, and perception checking as listening skills?
- Can you effectively use the verbal communication techniques of probing, reflecting, interpreting, confronting, informing, summarizing, self-disclosing, focusing, making observations, and suggesting?
- Do you know how to appropriately employ closed questions and facilitative questions and statements?
- Can you identify guidelines for giving clients feedback in learning and performance situations?
- Can you describe the importance of nonverbal communications in interacting with clients?
- Can you identify the major types of nonverbal communications?
- Are you familiar with proxemics?
- Are you able to give examples of how cultural differences play a role in nonverbal communications?
- Can you describe guidelines that would be helpful when communicating with clients with verbal or hearing impairments, or with clients who use wheelchairs or who speak foreign languages?
- Can you outline techniques for conducting a productive interview?

These questions outline some of the elements involved in therapeutic communication. They are drawn from the chapter on therapeutic communication in my book *Therapeutic Recreation Processes and Techniques* (Austin, 2009). I hope pondering this extensive list of questions will alert you to just how involved it is for any helping professional to become a competent communicator.

It is important to recognize that therapeutic communication skills are not arcane abilities limited to a select few professions such as clinical psychology, social work, or nursing. There is nothing esoteric about developing skills in therapeutic communication. In fact, being a competent communicator is a skill that every recreational therapist must develop.

Recreational therapy students typically have not had specific instruction in developing therapeutic communication techniques prior to entering their university professional preparation program. When they do begin to learn therapeutic communication techniques, they are sometimes surprised to discover that their newfound skills can be applied to enhance communications not just in clinical settings, but in all parts of their everyday lives.

In my textbook (Austin, 2009), I tell the story of Pam who was an undergraduate student of mine when I initially began teaching at Indiana University. I can still vividly recall Pam on the day she hurried into the therapeutic communication class I was teaching to announce with great glee that she had tried out with her friends some of the communication techniques we had practiced the prior class session and that they had worked for her. She went on to say that while the techniques had worked in class, she was surprised to find they worked with her friends as well.

Pam happened to one of the brightest students that it was my privilege to teach in my years at Indiana. Her disposition I would say was unassuming, and no one would describe her as being terribly outgoing.

Yet there she was that day, in front of the entire class, acting as excited as I had ever seen one of my students. I have to admit that I was caught off guard by her great exuberance for what had happened, as well as her expression of surprise that the verbal response techniques we went over in class were as effective in the Union Building snack bar as they had been in our classroom.

I use the story of Pam to illustrate that interpersonal communications skills gained through professional preparation in recreational therapy curricula are not some special, magical means of communicating that must be reserved for use only when interacting with clients in clinical practice. In fact, if you develop finely honed communications skills, you will find that many of them will serve you well not only in client communications but when interacting with other health care professions and, like Pam, in your everyday interactions with your friends and others.

The "bottom line" is that you should take the study of therapeutic communication skills very seriously. Like any other skill, it takes instruction, time, and practice to develop skills in therapeutic communication. But developing them is well worth the effort. In fact, without well-developed therapeutic communication skills, it is unlikely any recreational therapist will be effective.

Self-esteem can't be bestowed on clients by recreational therapists. Yet, as I have tried to demonstrate, there are a number of strategies that recreational therapists may employ to help clients to achieve greater self-esteem. All strategies call for clients themselves to gain from the responses of others, because self-esteem is something that clients achieve as a result of the positive feedback they receive from others.

My Favorite Approaches to Effective Listening

It has been said that "most people lack the skills to listen effectively" (Purtilo & Haddad, 2002, p. 182). If this is true (and I happen to think it is), it is necessary for all helping professionals, including recreational therapists, to build their listening skills.

There are no secretes to active listening as far as I know. But there are two things that I've found have helped me to become a better listener. These are: (1) using nonverbal behaviors effectively; and (2) employing verbal techniques that encourage clients to talk.

By nonverbal behaviors I mean eye contact, posture, and gestures. I will discuss all three because each is important.

Although in some cultures, eye contact is avoided as a way to defer to others, in America and Canada, eye contact generally serves as a way of signaling attention. Maintaining eye contact with the person indicates interest in what he or she is saying. Of course, by maintaining eye contact, I do not mean continually staring at the person. Contact should be broken every once in a while, but then it should once again be maintained.

Posture also is a way to show interest in the client who is talking. Whether sitting or standing, this is done by maintaining a relaxed position with a slight forward lean. The effective listener also avoids crossing his or her arms as this conveys being closed to what is being said.

The gesture that I personally favor is the use of head nods to indicate agreement or understanding. Otherwise, I just use normal hand gestures, and as I do so, I attempt to be as relaxed as possible as I gesture. For example, I don't gesture quickly or fidget.

In general, being relaxed is a key in effective listening. I don't want to do anything that will bring stress or tension to the client. I want the client to be as relaxed as possible so he or she can feel unencumbered in order to "open up" to me.

There are many verbal response techniques that can be used in effective listening. Perhaps I most commonly use paraphrasing (or restating what the client said in fewer words), clarifying (or asking the client to restate something I am unclear about), probing (or asking for additional information by saying something like, "Tell me more about that."), and summarizing (or drawing thoughts together at the end of a session).

My favorite verbal response technique ironically involves saying very little. This is the minimal verbal response when I say something like "yes," "I see," or "uh-huh," typically nodding my head at the same time. I find that this works well for me, because it reinforces the client without disrupting the flow of conversation.

I suppose another thing that the use of the minimal verbal technique does is to help me avoid cutting off the speaker. Early in my career, I had a tendency to not let clients complete their thoughts. I would jump in and disrupt their train of thought (probably due to my own nervousness). Perhaps the minimum verbal response technique helps me to avoid this personal pitfall.

There are, of course, many other verbal response techniques that can be used in active listening. These are covered in the chapter on communication skills in my book, *Therapeutic Recreation Processes and Techniques* (Austin, 2009) should you wish to review them.

It is my view that a good approach in the use of verbal response techniques is to get to know the full repertoire of verbal responses that can be used and then try them out. You will likely feel most comfortable in employing certain ones of these verbal responses because they seem to work for you. In my mind, it is fine to regularly draw upon those verbal responses in being an effective listener.

A final thought in regard to building effective listening skills is for you to hone those skills through practice. I believe that I have become a more effective listener simply because I have had many opportunities to use my skills.

Top Teaching Principles

Each fall in my Techniques in Therapeutic Recreation course, we would spend a class session talking about the 20 Teaching/Learning Principles covered in my textbook *Therapeutic Recreation: Processes and Techniques* (Austin, 2009). Following a review of each of the principles, class members would vote on which five principles they considered to be the most important.

It was amazing that every fall, year after year, the student vote was almost always identical. The students tended to select as their top five principles: (1) Start at the level of the client and move at a rate that is comfortable, (2) Individual differences must be given consideration, (3) Reinforcement strengthens learning, (4) Active engagement and participation are essential for learning, and (5) Move from the simple to the complex.

I'm really not sure why there was so much consistency from year to year in my students choosing what they perceived to be the most important teaching/learning principles. I do believe in the collective wisdom of students, so I believe it is worth devoting this lesson to a review of the most important teaching/learning principles as selected by my students.

It is possible that the students selected the principle, "Start at the level of the client and move at a rate that is comfortable," just because it is perhaps the teaching/learning principle that most people have been exposed to. I think most of us have heard that in teaching it is important to not be too much above your students' levels and not to advance too fast or they will be overwhelmed and lose interest. We have also been told that we shouldn't be below our students' levels and not to go too slowly, or they will become bored and lose interest. This advice may be commonly known, but this doesn't detract from the principle. Instead, the wide acceptance of the principle provides a kind of "face validity" for it.

"Individual differences must be given consideration" is a teaching/learning principle that may appeal intuitively to emerging recreational therapists. They know it is critical to conduct an assessment of every client since they realize that each client possesses unique strengths and interests. This approach leads to the natural conclusion that each client is unique and therefore will learn in a unique fashion.

The idea that "reinforcement strengthens learning" is certainly one that has been around for some time. The underlying notion behind this principle is that people tend to repeat (i.e., learn) those behaviors that bring them rewards. Rewards may come in the form of social reinforcers such as approval or attention. To master a new skill can, in itself, be intrinsically rewarding as people feel the joy of accomplishment. Even extrinsic rewards can strengthen people's tendency to do something. Things like trophies, money, and even candy can serve as extrinsic rewards.

"Active engagement and participation are essential for learning" is a teaching/learning principle that has a great fit with recreational therapy, because recreational therapy is all about experiential learning or learning by doing. Clients take part in recreational therapy activities that they have selected because they really enjoy doing them or, at the least, anticipate positive outcomes from taking part. The positive attitudes clients hold toward their participation leads them to deep levels of involvement. I believe we would all agree that we learn better when we are really "into" something.

"Move from the simple to the complex" is the fifth and last principle identified by the students. I suppose this principle could be rephrased to read "move from the familiar to the unfamiliar," or "go from the concrete to abstract." The point is to start with the basics and proceed from there. Of course, being mindful of the teaching/learning principle that suggests we start at the level of the client, we need to be sure not to be too simple or too basic or we may insult our learner.

I very much like all five of the teaching/learning principles typically selected by my students. But each year after my students had their say, I would share with them my personal favorite among the 20 teaching/learning principles found in my book.

That favorite is to "relate new learning to existing knowledge." I've long held that learning occurs when we make a personal connection between what we already know and what we have learned. This is the moment we make it our own. In fact, I think it could be said that the personalization of information is learning. Making the connection between what we already know and something new personalizes the learning. The personal connection produces the "eureka moment" or experience when "the light bulb goes on." This is the time when we "get it."

So to me, it is critical that the recreational therapist finds something that the client can connect with in terms of new learning. The connection exists between what the client already knows or a previously learned skill and the new knowledge or skill. It may be as simple as building on a skill the client already possesses, such as the throwing motion when throwing a ball and then connecting this motion with learning the new motion of a tennis serve.

I developed my initial list of teaching/learning principles back in the early 1970s when I was working on my Ph.D. It was my intent to codify or systematically organize what was known about teaching and learning into a single list of principles. Over the years, I have refined and enlarged the list as I encountered additional principles that I thought could be useful in the teaching/learning process. I hope that sharing what my students and I perceive to be the most important teaching/learning principles will prove helpful to you. Should you wish to explore my entire list of 20 principles I would invite you to read the section in my textbook (Austin, 2009) on teaching/learning principles.

Recreational Therapists as Applied Social Psychologists

Recreational therapy is a social enterprise directed toward helping clients to change their behaviors, thoughts, and feelings. At the minimum, recreational therapy involves interactions between the recreational therapist and client. More often recreational therapy transpires in groups where a multitude of social influences can occur. Thus, recreational therapy involves a knowledge and appreciation of interpersonal dynamics.

Where do recreational therapists gain knowledge and appreciation of the interpersonal dynamics they deal with every day? It seems to me that an obvious answer is that they are gained through social psychology. After all, social psychology deals with the social aspects of human behavior—how people's actions, thoughts, and feelings are affected by others.

When I was doing my Ph.D. at the University of Illinois, one of my professors called those of us in recreational therapy "applied social psychologists." He felt we were about applying understandings from social psychology to recreational therapy. We students liked the notion of being called "applied social psychologists" and took some measure of pride in being labeled such.

I believe my professor was on to something when he termed us "applied social psychologists." He understood that those of us in recreational therapy were fascinated by social psychology, because time and time again we could use research and theory from social psychology to understand the social interactions we saw occurring in recreational therapy.

You have to look no further than the table of contents of any introductory textbook in social psychology to understand how those topics of interest to social psychologists are ones that recreational therapists are vitally interested in. Tables of contents might likely include such topics as: self-concepts; attitudes; persuasion and attitude change; attributional processes; prejudice and discrimination; self-presentation; aggression; prosocial behavior; conformity, compliance, and obedience; and group processes.

Mark Leary (see Leary & Miller, 1986, and Kowalski & Leary, 1999) has written extensively about the interface of social psychology and clinical psychology. Leary's work establishes strong links between social and clinical psychology and how understandings from social psychology can be applied in clinical psychology.

I believe there is no question that Leary is right that clinicians dealing with emotional and behavioral problems can use understandings from social psychology in their work. Yet, I would suggest that understandings from social psychology are not restricted to applications in clinical psychology. I believe knowledge from social psychology can be applied to serving virtually every client group with whom recreational therapists work, not just within mental health.

An obvious example is group processes. The majority of recreational therapy is provided within group settings. Therefore, it behooves recreational therapists to know basic group dynamics so they can interpret behaviors within groups and facilitate the group as leaders.

Another obvious example of an area from social psychology that can be used within recreational therapy deals with attitudes and attitude change. Recreational therapists regularly work with many different types of clients to bring about attitude change in areas such as leisure, fitness, and self-attitudes (e.g., self-esteem).

Still another example of borrowing from social psychology deals with attributional processes. Almost all recreational therapists have studied the theory of learned helplessness and therefore know how feelings of learned helplessness can lead to apathy, withdrawal, and depression. Most recreational therapy students also have been exposed to Langer and Rodin's (1976) classic nursing home study in which learned helplessness was overted for residents who were given relatively minor opportunities to exercise control over their environments.

I hope from these examples involving group processes, attitudes, and attributional processes that you can see how social psychology can be applied in recreational therapy. In fact, by now I would be surprised if you can't construct your own examples of how understandings from social psychology can be applied in recreational therapy.

It was my good fortune to have professors in my Ph.D. program that helped me to see the close connections between social psychology and recreational therapy. I now want to share that realization with you. Whether you are an emerging recreational therapist or a seasoned recreational therapist, there is much in social psychology that can be of benefit to you.

If you are still in college, make sure you take at least an introductory course in social psychology. If you are doing graduate study, arrange to take a social psychology course. I can think of no better minor for a Ph.D. student in recreational therapy than social psychology. Even if you are not in school or have no plans to seek an advanced degree, you can study social psychology by taking a course or through reading. The Kowalski and Leary (1999) book is one good reference, or you may wish to read an article I authored for the *1991 Annual in Therapeutic Recreation* titled "The Interface Between Social and Clinical Psychology: Implications for Therapeutic Recreation."

I hope that each of you will begin to gain and use understandings from social psychology within recreational therapy. If you do, you too may wish to proudly proclaim yourself to be "an applied social psychologist."

The Overjustification Effect

What if you were to give children a reward for doing something they already enjoy doing? Will they tend to like the activity more, less, or about the same?

Knowing about a famous social psychology study by Mark Lepper and his colleagues can be of a great deal of help to recreational therapists in answering this question. Lepper, Greene, and Nisbett (1973) showed that children who were given an expected reward for play behaviors they naturally enjoyed (playing with magic markers) were less likely to subsequently participate in that play behavior.

The tendency for intrinsic motivation to diminish for activities that become associated with reward is known as the "overjustification effect." This is because rewards are unneeded incentives to bring about behaviors that would be done voluntarily without any incentives and, in fact, result in lessening intrinsic motivation.

It should be noted that the decrease in intrinsic motivation just pertains to instances where people know they will be rewarded and they receive the expected reward. The overjustification effect does not hold when people receive a reward without the prior promise of a reward accompanying their actions.

The overjustification effect is counterintuitive in that we typically believe that rewards will increase behaviors. We tend to think if someone receives a reward for doing something that he or she will be more likely to repeat that behavior. Lepper's research has shown this not to be true in cases where rewards are promised for doing something that is intrinsically motivated behavior.

Unfortunately, some recreational therapists evidently have not learned about the overjustification effect. On many occasions, I have personally viewed recreational therapists indiscriminately promising and distributing rewards to clients for taking part in an activity, even though the clients love participating in the activity for its own sake.

The important thing to remember is that rewards can undermine intrinsic motivation if people are told they will receive them for participating in an activity. We can turn recreation into work by "paying off" people for doing something they already enjoy doing.

Recreational therapists need to be careful not to take something that is an enjoyable, intrinsically motivated activity and turn it to be something the person will be only extrinsically motivated to do. We generally want clients to participate in activities for their own enjoyment, not for the reward it will get them.

On the other hand, recreational therapists need to recall that the overjustification effect does not hold when the reward is not promised in advance. Also, social psychologists

Brehm, Kassin, and Steven Fein (2005) have pointed out that, if the reward is sincere verbal praise or viewed as a special bonus for an exceptional performance, it can actually enhance intrinsic motivation when it comes from a respected person. This is because the reward is construed as providing positive feedback about the performer's competence.

So the bottom line is that while giving clients rewards can be a good approach, it can also backfire if the recreational therapist promises clients rewards for doing something they already like to do.

Self-Efficacy

Why Some Clients Try and Others Don't

When I was a young recreational therapist, I often would get angry at my clients because they would not even try activities that I knew would be good for them. I wish I had been exposed to Albert Bandura's (1986, 1997) self-efficacy theory at that time, because it would have allowed me to have a better understanding of my clients and what likely caused what I saw as simply negative behavior.

The fact is that clients' beliefs that they can succeed at a task play a crucial role in whether they pursue rehabilitative activities or not. If clients believe they are capable of carrying something out they will attempt it; if not they won't. In fact, if they do not believe they have the capabilities to succeed, they may avoid even attempting the particular act (as my clients did).

Bandura (1997) has termed individuals' learned beliefs in their capabilities of carrying out a specific behavior or attaining a desired outcome as their levels of perceived self-efficacy. Self-efficacy deals with beliefs about being able to execute a specific behavior (e.g., becoming physically fit), rather than having a general level of self-confidence. Those high in self-efficacy feel they are competent to carry out a specific action and expect to be successful in carrying it out. They therefore will persist in the face of challenges because they believe they can succeed in accomplishing a specific action.

High self-efficacy produces what might be termed a kind of self-fulfilling prophecy. If you really believe you can do something, the harder you will try, and the greater will be the likelihood for success.

All recreational therapists have had clients with high self-efficacy. These clients want to overcome their health concerns and believe they can achieve success by following the specific path they have laid out with the recreational therapist. All recreational therapists have also had clients with low self-efficacy. These clients tend to give up easily, or they may not even try at all. Almost all recreational therapists have had clients who would not attempt an activity because they feared that they would fail. This is dysfunctional behavior, because by avoiding participation they limit their opportunities for success—which is what they need to increase their feelings of self-efficacy!

An example of such dysfunctional behavior has been provided by Leary and Miller (1986) who discussed a young female client who was so shy she avoided contact because she lacked social competence or because she believed that no matter how she interacted with others that she would be rejected.

How do clients increase their self-efficacy or their judgments that they can perform well enough to accomplish some end? Perhaps the greatest source of increasing self-efficacy is through direct participation in doing something and feeling successful in doing it. Feeling successful on a number of occasions will likely produce increases in self-efficacy. It has been suggested it is best to build from initial small successes when offering opportunities for mastery experiences that allow a sense of personal accomplishment. The task difficulty levels can be increased as client abilities develop and confidence grows. (Austin, 2009)

Of course, engaging in activities may be difficult for those with extremely low self-efficacy. They will probably not wish to attempt something in which they believe they lack competence.

In such cases, the recreational therapist will first have to have confidence that the client can be successful. Then the therapist will need to be persuasive in urging the client to attempt to succeed. Verbal persuasion from the recreational therapist is one key to getting the client to take part.

Another means to increase self-efficacy is through vicarious experiences. Seeing others like them gain success may raise their beliefs in their own capacities. "If he can do it, so can I," is the thinking that should be encouraged.

A final means to increasing self-efficacy is helping the client in achieving a relatively relaxed physiological state. Feeling less arousal can have a calming effect and produce more positive expectations (Bandura, 1986). Stress-reduction techniques (e.g., deep breathing, progressive relaxation training, meditation, yoga) offer one means to reduce feelings of arousal.

Self-efficacy theory provides recreational therapists a means to understand client behaviors. It also offers means to enhance feelings of self-efficacy. Let's hope recreational therapists become acquainted with Bundura's (1986, 1997) self-efficacy theory so it may become more widely applied in recreational therapy.

Social Facilitation

There are social phenomena that I have sometimes figured out for myself and later read information in the literature of social psychology that supported my original thinking. Social facilitation is one of those concepts that I knew about as a result of working with my clients at a state hospital in Indiana.

Social facilitation is the phenomenon in which the presence of others leads to improvement in performance. This phenomenon I saw when my clients would rehearse for a performance, such as a hospital variety show. The clients would do a good job in rehearsals, but when the lights came on in front of an audience of hundreds they would perform exceptionally! The presence of an audience facilitated or enhanced the clients' performances.

It is ironic that the first scientific research on social facilitation also took place in Indiana (as had my first experience with social facilitation). Professor Norman Triplett (1897) of Indiana University found that the racing times for bicyclists were faster when they performed with other bicyclists rather than racing against time. Like my clients, the bicycle riders' performance was improved by the presence of others.

By the way, Triplett's social facilitation research is commonly cited as the first recorded study in the history of social psychology. Unfortunately, Triplett's study did not explain the dynamics as to exactly why the presence of others affected performance.

Luckily for us, a psychologist by the name of Robert Zajonc (1965) was able to come up with an explanation as to why performances are affected by the presence of others. His explanation was that the presence of others raises our general level of emotional arousal, and this elevates performance.

However, the notion of social facilitation theory that the presence of others improves performances did not seem to account for those instances where the presence of others seemed to have a deteriorating effect on how people performed. Zajonc had an answer for this as well.

What he explained was that emotional arousal has an enhancing affect on people when they perform well-learned tasks – but emotional arousal diminishes performance levels with poorly-learned tasks. In order words, the dominant response comes out when emotional arousal is experienced. Some refer to the enhancing effect as social facilitation and the diminishing effect as social inhibition.

What, may you ask, has all this to do with recreational therapy? This is a fair question.

The implications are that we should seek opportunities for our clients to perform well-learned tasks with others. Thus, once they have learned something well they should do it with others. For example, if they have learned a recreational skill, they should be encouraged to do it with others.

One the other hand, if they are just learning a new skill it may be best for them to learn it in a one-to-one learning environment with the recreational therapist or, at the least, in a small group. Because it is not a well-learned skill the presence of others is likely to interfere with their performance.

Other studies have led social psychologists to understand that the phenomenon of social facilitation is more complex than even Zajonc thought (Brehm, Kassin, & Fein, 2005). But discussion of these complexities is beyond the bounds of this chapter.

So just remember that the presence of others will be likely to: (a) enhance performance of skills that are well-learned (which are often easier skills); and (b) interfere with performance of skills that are not well-learned (often more difficult skills). And, as a result, put your clients in situations where well-learned skills will be enhanced by the presence of others and keep clients away from others when they are first developing their skills.

Self-Handicapping

As a young recreational therapist, I often saw my clients giving half-hearted efforts when taking part in activities. I wondered why this was. Why would my clients not really try? My guesses for their lack of effort ranged from just being plain lazy to being made groggy as a side-effect of their medications. Later, in graduate school, I discovered an answer as to why many of my clients did not seem to try when they were participating in recreational therapy activities. The reason was that they were probably self-handicapping.

What exactly is self-handicapping? It is the term given to instances where people actually sabotage their own performance. They handicap themselves by building a ready excuse in case they fail at something. For example, a coed may "pull an all-nighter" in order to have the ready excuse of being exhausted if she fails an important exam. This excuse offers a self-esteem protecting explanation for lacking the ability to do well on the exam.

Do our clients ever participate in self-handicapping to protect their egos? Yes, I would suggest that was exactly what was happening when, as a young recreational therapist, my clients didn't really try when participating in activities. By not giving it their all, they could claim that they really didn't try so their lack of success could be attributed to their self-handicapping excuse rather than a lack of ability.

While not giving a full effort is not a terrible thing in itself, it is too bad, because clients obviously will not get the benefits from their participation that they might have if they had actually given it their best. Self-handicapping can become a serious problem when people do things like drinking great quantities of alcohol before an important event so they can blame their poor performance on the effects of their drinking. Others may become chronic underachievers by always giving less than their best because of their doubts about their abilities. In fact, they may never know just how much they are capable of achieving.

A related phenomenon is self-reported handicap when people don't actually do anything to have a ready excuse for their lack of performance. Instead, they just make up an excuse to cover themselves. An example would be chronically using illness as an excuse for not performing well. Perhaps you even have friends who never seem to feel well enough "to be at their best." When such friends are always telling you their health problems have prevented them from performing well, they are engaging in self-reported handicapping.

It is important that recreational therapists know about self-handicapping and self-reported handicap. If I had know of self-handicapping when I was a young recreational therapist I could have realized my clients were trying to save face by not giving it their all while participating in activities. Knowing this, I could have provided additional support or encouragement in order to get them to participate more fully. I also could have known that perhaps their self-esteem was fragile and needed bolstering.

Becoming aware of the phenomena of self-handicapping and self-report handicap can also prove to be helpful to each of us when examining our own behavior. Do we ever engage in such behaviors to protect our self-esteem? My guess is that most of us have. Knowing of these behaviors we can choose to use more adaptive means to maintain our self-esteem.

The information for this lesson has primarily been drawn from my book, *Therapeutic Recreation Processes and Techniques* (Austin, 2009). You may wish to refer to my book for further information on self-handicapping and self-report handicap.

Self-Fulfilling Prophecy

When we have expectations about what others are like, we can inadvertently and unconsciously behave in ways consistent with our expectations, which causes those persons to behave consistently with our expectations. When others' characteristics meet our expectations due how we interact with them, this is termed a self-fulfilling prophecy.

In my book (Austin, 2009) I have provided the example of a recreational therapist who engaged in self-fulfilling prophecy. He had the preformed expectation of members of his recreational therapy group that they could not take care of themselves. He therefore treated them in a condescending way. His approach led the group members to become dependent. Thus, the recreational therapist was able to confirm his preformed expectation. The group members acted in accord with his expectations of them and of the way he treated them!

A better illustration of the self-fulfilling prophecy is the classic "bloomers" study completed by Rosenthal and Jacobson (1968). In their study, these researchers randomly selected students as being "bloomers." The researchers then told the teacher that according to testing they had done that these students would "bloom" or spurt ahead of other students. A year later, further testing revealed that those students identified to the teacher as bloomers did in fact achieve at a significantly higher level than the other students in the class.

How did this happen? The explanation had to be that the teacher's expectations that the students identified as "bloomers" would do better was confirmed as a result of the way she treated those students during the year, in contrast to how she treated the "nonbloomers."

According to Aronson, Wilson, and Akert (1999), later research has revealed that teachers with preconceived expectations of students who they thought had the ability to achieve (i.e., "bloomers") behaved in ways that elicited the expected behavior. For those they expected to achieve, the teachers created a warmer social climate by giving them more personal attention and encouragement. They also gave these students more material to learn and more difficult material. Additionally, the teachers rewarded those they expected to achieve with greater and more positive feedback than other students received. Finally, they allowed these students more opportunities to perform in class than they gave the other students.

I believe that as a university professor, I generally held my students in high regard and had the expectation that they would be capable of achieving at a high level. I believe that having positive preconceived expectations of my students that this affected their abilities to perform at a high level. I believe I got what I expected from my students.

In my personal experience, I believe the self-fulfilling prophecy worked to my students' advantage. Sometimes, however, this is not the case. Negative expectations can have adverse affects on those who are the target of preconceived expectations. For example, instead of holding positive expectations of my students, if I were to hold negative expectations, it could erode their confidence and have a damaging effect on their performance.

I am sure you can easily see the ramifications of the self-fulfilling prophecy within recreational therapy. It behooves us to hold positive expectations of our clients. In so doing, we will likely treat our clients as if they can and will enjoy success.

Learned Helplessness

Have you ever heard someone say, "It doesn't matter how hard I try, I'll never be able to satisfy that professor," or "I could stay here until doomsday and not ever be able to understand statistics. I give up."

We could speculate that those saying these things are likely experiencing learned helplessness. People experiencing learned helplessness believe that no matter what they do, they don't have the power or control to achieve positive outcomes. They enter a state of pessimism in which they see themselves as inadequate to control outcomes no matter how much they try. They perceive the situation to be futile and themselves as helpless to do anything about it.

When people become "learned helpless," it is debilitating. They perceive that it doesn't matter what they do, they can't succeed. Everything is out of their control. So they simply give up. Such feelings of helplessness can make people apathetic. What is there to care about if nothing you do matters?

More problematic is that helplessness can lead to withdrawal and depression. People may withdraw in order to isolate themselves from what they see as a negative environment. Or they may become depressed as they simply give up due to the perceived sense of uncontrollability over the environment that they are experiencing. They may think: "I'm no good. I can't do anything. What is the sense of trying? I'm just continually beating my head against the wall. I just simply give up." Such thinking naturally can lead to deep feelings of depression.

Psychologist Martin Seligman's (1975) classic studies with animals, and later with humans, brought to the forefront the notion that learned helplessness can lead to depression. But perhaps Langer and Rodin's (1976) classic nursing home study is the research that is most cited in the literature of recreational therapy. These researchers found that allowing residents to make relatively little decisions (e.g., about which night to view a movie) or take small responsibilities (e.g., being responsible for watering a plant) provided residents a sense of control in the nursing home environment in which they typically lacked control. The impact of gaining a sense of control was profound. Residents exhibited behaviors that were the opposite of being learned helpless as they became more alert, participated more in activities, and in general exhibited a greater sense of well-being.

Today it is widely documented that controlling institutional environments can lead to learned helplessness (see Voelkl, 1986). Because recreational therapy offers the antithesis of the controlling environments often found in institutional environments, such as hospitals and nursing homes, it can offer clients a sense of control and prevent feelings of learned helplessness as clients are provided opportunities to make decisions and assume responsibilities while interacting with recreational therapists who strive to create an optimistic atmosphere (Austin, 2009).

Evidence-Based Practice
A Concept RT Should Embrace

Evidence-based practice (EBP) is a concept that has risen to the forefront in healthcare in the past decade. The idea of EBP is to use the best evidence available when making decisions about the care and treatment of each individual client by integrating the latest empirical research findings and other reliable evidence with the therapist's clinical expertise. Integrating the best available external evidence with the therapist's clinical experience allows the delivery of quality care to the greatest extent possible.

EBP means knowing and following research and reliable clinical evidence that tells you what to do. EBP also means knowing and following research and reliable clinical evidence that informs you what *not* to do. Most of all, EBP means not following out-of-date information or doing things a certain way because you have always done them that way even though you have never given your approach thoughtful analysis. The variability in recreational therapy clinical approaches today is dramatic due to a lack of evidence-based practice. This lack is for three primary reasons it seems to me.

One reason is that a broader acceptance of EBP is required within the recreational therapy profession. This acceptance needs to encompass both faculty in university recreational therapy programs and practitioners on the front lines.

A second reason for a lack of EBP in recreational therapy is that there is a pressing need for more and better evidence on what RT interventions work best for which clients. Both our research base and reliable clinical approach base need to be improved and expanded.

The third reason why EBP has not caught on in recreational therapy is that a lack of means exist to accelerate the dissemination of new knowledge. Dissemination systems are not available to reach a wide spectrum of practitioners.

What can we do to bring about greater acceptance and use of EBP within the recreational therapy community? I don't claim to have all the answers to this question, but I wish to raise some ideas that may serve as food for thought for improving the situation that exists today, so that EBP may become an integral part of recreational therapy.

Academic programs in recreational therapy have the potential to lead the EBP movement. University faculty should keep up with the latest developments in healthcare practice and therefore have a solid understanding of evidence-based practice and the need for it to be embraced within recreational therapy. In short, faculty would seem to be the natural leaders to provide the initial advocacy for EBP. Faculty advocacy should begin in the classroom as instructors inform students about EBP and then provide examples of how EBP can be employed in the field.

Other roles for university faculty are those of scholars and researchers. As scholars, faculty should author literature that presents the latest research and clinical findings so that this information is available to the field. As researchers, faculty need to produce practice-based research. Faculty should work closely with practitioners in the field to collect and record data on interventions and outcomes.

University faculty may also take leadership roles when it comes to instructional technology (IT) because universities often possess information technology systems that can reach out to those in the field. Such information technology systems must be developed in order to get up-to-date clinical evidence out to the front lines so it is accessible to busy practitioners. In our electronic age, there does not seem to be a good reason why recreational therapy practice information should not be made available to those practitioners via IT so that they may make informed decisions.

You may be asking yourself, "What roles should recreational therapy practitioners play when it comes to EBP?" One obvious step would be for practitioners to join with university faculty to collaborate in doing clinical research. While faculty may take the lead in setting up research protocols, practitioners are invaluable partners for faculty conducting clinical research.

A related role for practitioners is sharing their clinical expertise in terms of informing other practitioners of their clinical successes. While such clinical practice information is not strictly formal research, it may be highly valuable to other practitioners who are dealing with similar situations. Such information sharing may take several forms. One is authoring articles for professional newsletters or journals that are read by other practitioners. A second means is making presentations at workshops and conferences. Still another means to sharing clinical information is becoming a part of a networking group that shares clinical information at meetings or through electronic data sharing.

Professional associations likewise can play a key role in bringing EBP into the mainstream of recreational therapy. For instance, associations can make sure that they offer insights for their members on the importance of EBP and also provide continuing education opportunities for practitioners to gain clinical expertise from researchers and other practitioners. Additionally, professional associations can work with universities in establishing information technology systems to disseminate the best available clinical evidence to practitioners.

Before closing this lesson, it is worth mentioning that evidence-based practice may be a bit more complex than it seems at first blush. Both university professional preparation programs and professional associations need to impress on practitioners that EBP is not as straightforward as it may seem. Practitioners can't just take the latest clinical research findings or reliable clinical approaches and apply them with their clients.

Even with practice grounded in an evidence base, we have to personalize the approach for every client. Clients with similar diagnoses may present very different cases due to their ages, the strengths they possess, available social support systems, cultural backgrounds, their attitudes toward treatment, and so on. Also to be taken into consideration when using EBP are the clinical skills and experiences of the therapist. If the therapist does not have the clinical expertise to apply a certain clinical approach, the therapist should not attempt to use it. Having stated these warnings, EBP is a concept whose time has come for recreational therapy. The recreational therapy profession should move with haste to make EBP a regular part of its practice.

As a footnote to this lesson, I should tell you that while I have believed in evidence-based practice for many years, I have been heavily influenced by the writings on EBP by my former colleagues at Indiana University. My former colleagues, professors Youngkhill Lee, Bryan McCormick, and Marieke Van Puymbroeck have done a great deal in recent years to advance EBP in recreational therapy (e.g., see McCormick, Lee, & Van Puymbroeck, 2009; Lee & McCormick, 2002).

My current thinking on EBP has been further stimulated by the Institute of Medicine publication titled *Evidence-Based Medicine and the Changing Nature of Healthcare* (McClellan, McGinnis, Nabel, & Olsen, 2008). I would commend this insightful work to anyone wishing to pursue the topic further.

Say "Yes" to RT Research

In my practitioner days, if you told me I would someday be writing a chapter for a book about overcoming fears of RT research, I might have thought you were out of your mind! As a young professional, I could have cared less about research. I had taken no research courses as an undergraduate. I took only one research course as a master's student, and it didn't "take."

Research was not on my practitioner radar. I knew little about it, and what I did know seemed scary and intimidating. Research was something for those smart guys in the psychology department on the hospital's first floor, not for us fun-loving recreational therapists down in our basement office.

If the word "research" has you quaking in your boots, join the club! Most recreational therapists seem to have a fear of research. After all, we recreational therapists join our profession because we want to help people through direct care, not because we want to engage in scholarly inquiry. It is natural that research might seem outside of our comfort zones.

Now, many years later, I actually get excited about recreational therapy research. To make discoveries through research is something special. It is extremely satisfying on a personal level to be able to conceptualize a study, collect data, and come up with positive findings. Then you get to share what you have learned with others. Typically this is done by first presenting your findings to other researchers and then publishing your findings in a journal. Ultimately you hope your research will make a difference in the delivery of recreational therapy services.

There wasn't much attention given to research by our profession when I began my career as a recreational therapist. Things have changed a great deal over the course of my career that has spanned some 45 years. Happily today, with the emphasis on evidence-based practice, research has taken a prominent place in recreational therapy. We now recognize the importance of research.

My personal conversion to research came when I entered the Ph.D. program at the University of Illinois. Illinois is a true research university; research is highly valued there. The head of our department of leisure studies at Illinois was Professor Al Sapora. Dr. Sapora knew that to become accepted as an academic discipline that our department had to display to others on campus that it, too, could produce quality research.

So to establish the department as a valid academic enterprise, Dr. Sapora set about to bring in faculty who could be productive scholars. The progressive group of "young turks" he brought in included Professors Doyle Bishop, Rainer Martens, and Mike Ellis. These men sought to set a new, higher standard for research in recreation and leisure.

Cherish the Opportunity to Do Recreational Therapy

We in recreational therapy are in envious positions. First and foremost, we are able to help others in need. There is a great deal of gratification in being able to help others.

Many times we help only in small ways. Occasionally, however, what we do may be life changing. I think what is important is that we have the opportunity to touch the lives of others and make a difference in their lives.

It is a wonderful thing to see our clients overcoming barriers to health, fulfilling their potentials, and achieving meaningful lives that lead them to feelings of well-being and contentment. I don't know of anything that can top those feelings of having played a part in helping someone to surmount obstacles to health so that they may enjoy a rewarding life.

Of course, in always focusing on meeting the needs of others, their needs transcend our needs. Continually putting others first can be difficult. This is especially true when we are emerging recreational therapists. In fact, I would have to say that many emerging recreational therapists find it exceedingly hard to always put their clients first. Yet most will learn to adapt to making the needs of others primary. This is the nature of the helping relationship. It is a hazard of being a helping professional.

I've always felt that despite putting our clients first that we recreational therapists have advantages that most other helping professionals do not enjoy. Our focus on the positive is very unique within the helping professions. We recreational therapists have always been optimists, full of hope, who believe in the capacity of clients to change. We emphasize our clients' abilities and capitalize on our clients' strengths to create positive emotional outcomes such as fun, enjoyment, and satisfaction. Because of our positive approach, clients tend to get attached to us. They like us and what we do with them.

I hope you will feel very lucky, very blessed to have chosen to become a recreational therapist. Our profession is a special one. It is one that is to be cherished.

References

Aronson, A., Wilson, T. D., & Akert, R. M. (1999). *Social psychology* (3ʳᵈ edition). New York: Longman.

Austin, D. R. (1986). Clinical supervision in therapeutic recreation. *Expanding Horizons in Therapeutic Recreation, 1*, 7–13.

Austin, D.R. (2002a). Conceptual models in therapeutic recreation. In D. R. Austin, J. Dattilo, & B. P. McCormick (Eds.). *Conceptual foundations for therapeutic recreation.* State College, PA: Venture.

Austin, D. R. (2002b). Control: A major element in therapeutic recreation. In D.R. Austin, J. Dattilo, & B.P. McCormick (Eds.). *Conceptual foundations for therapeutic recreation.* State College, PA: Venture.

Austin, D. R. (1998). The Health Protection/Health Promotion Model. *Therapeutic Recreation Journal, 32*, 109 – 117.

Austin, D. R. (1991). The interface between social and clinical psychology: Implications for therapeutic recreation. *Annual in Therapeutic Recreation, 2*, 59–68.

Austin, D. R. (2009). *Therapeutic recreation: Processes and techniques* (6ᵗʰ ed.). Champaign, IL: Sagamore.

Bandura, A. (1986). *Social foundations of thought and action: A social cognitive theory.* Englewood Cliffs, NJ: Prentice-Hall.

Bandura, A. (1997). *Self-efficacy: The exercise of control.* New York: W. H. Freeman and Company.

Biswas-Diener, R., & Dean, B. (2007). *Positive psychology coaching: Putting the science of happiness to work for your clients.* Hoboken, NJ: John Wiley & Sons.

Brehm, S. S., Kassin, S., & Fein, S. (2005). *Social psychology* (6ᵗʰ ed.). Boston: Houghton Mifflin Company.

Brill, N. I., & Levine, J. (2002). *Working with people: The helping process* (7ᵗʰ ed.). Boston: Allyn and Bacon.

Cain, D. J. (2002). Defining characteristics, history, and evolution of humanistic psychotherapies. In D. J. Cain (Ed.), *Humanistic psychotherapies: Handbook of research and practice.* Washington, D.C.: American Psychological Association, pp. 3–54.

Corey, G. (1995). *Theory and practice of group counseling* (4ᵗʰ ed.). Pacific Grove, CA: Brooks/Cole Publishing Company.

Corey, M.S., & Corey, G. (2006). *Groups: Process and practice* (7ᵗʰ ed.). Pacific Grove, CA: Thomson Brooks/Cole.

Dumas, R. G. (1994). Psychiatric nursing in an era of change. *Journal of Psychosocial Nursing, 32*(1), 11 – 14.

Flexner, A. (2001). Is social work a profession? *Research in Social Work Practice, 11*(2), 152–165.

Fredrickson, B. (2001). The role of positive emotions in positive psychology: The broaden-and-build theory of positive emotion. *American Psychologist, 56*, 218 – 226.

Gergen, K. J., & Gergen, M. M. (1986). *Social psychology* (2ⁿᵈ ed.). New York: Springer Verlag.

Glicken, M. D. (2004). *Using the strengths perspective in social work practice: A positive approach for the helping professional.* Boston: Pearson.

Grube, G.M.A. (1995). *The Greek and Roman critics.* Indianapolis: Hackett.

Gruver, B. M., & Austin, D. R. (1990). The instructional status of clinical supervision in therapeutic recreation curricula. *Therapeutic Recreation Journal, 24*(2), 18–24.

Haidt, J. (2006). *The happiness hypothesis.* New York: Basic Books.

Hall, K. J. (1997). Carl Rogers. Retrieved 2-15-09 from http://www.muskingum. edu/~psych/psychweb/history/rogers.htm

Hemingway, J. L. (1996). Emancipating leisure: The recovery of freedom in leisure. *Journal of Leisure Research, 28*(1), 27–43.

Hemingway, J. L. (1988). Leisure and civility: Reflections on a Greek ideal. *Leisure Sciences, 10*, 179 – 191.

Iso-Ahola, S. E. (1980). *The social psychology of leisure and recreation.* Dubuque: Wm. C. Brown.

Jin, B., & Austin, D. R. (2000). Personality types of therapeutic recreation students based on the MBTI. *Therapeutic Recreation Journal, 34*(1), 33 – 41.

Johansson, I., & Lynoe, N. (2008). *Medicine and philosophy: A twenty-first century introduction.* Piscataway, NJ: Transaction Books.

Jones, D. B., & Anderson, L. S. (2004). The status of clinical supervision in therapeutic recreation: A national study. *Therapeutic Recreation Journal, 38*(4), 329–342.

Kielhofner, G. (1997). *Conceptual foundations of occupational therapy* (2nd ed.). Philadelphia: F.A. Davis Company.

Kowalski, R. M., & Leary, M. R. (Eds.). (1999). *The social psychology of emotional and behavioral problems: Interfaces of social and clinical psychology.* Washington, D.C.: American Psychological Association.

Langer, E. B., & Rodin, J. (1976). The effects of choice and enhanced personal responsibility for the aged: A field experiment in an institutional setting. *Journal of Personality and Social Psychology, 34*, 191–198.

Leary, M. R. (1999). The social and psychological importance of self-esteem. In R. M. Kowalski, & M. R. Leary (Eds.), *The social psychology of emotional and behavioral problems: Interfaces of social and clinical psychology.* Washington, D.C.: American Psychological Association, pp. 197–221.

Leary, M. R., & Miller, R. S. (1986). *Social psychology and dysfunctional behavior: Origins, diagnosis, and treatment.* New York: Springer-Verlag.

Leary, M. R., Tambor, E. S., Terdal, S. K., & Downs, D. L. (1995). Self-esteem as an interpersonal monitor: The sociometer hypothesis. *Journal of Personality and Social Psychology, 68*(3), 518–530.

Lepper, M. R., Greene, D., & Nisbett, R. E. (1973). Undermining children's intrinsic interest with extrinsic rewards: A test of the "overjustification" hypothesis. *Journal of Personality and Social Psychology, 28*, 129–137.

Linley, P. A., & Joseph, S. (2004). *Positive psychology in practice.* Hoboken, NJ: John Wiley & Sons.

Marcum, J. A. (2008). *An introductory philosophy of medicine.* New York: Springer.

Maslach, C. (1982). *Burnout: The cost of caring.* Englewood Cliffs, NJ: Prentice-Hall.

Miller, W. R., & Rollnick, S. (1991). *Motivational interviewing: Preparing people to change addictive behavior.* New York: The Guilford Press.

Ornstein, R., & Sobel, D. (1989). *Healthy pleasures.* New York: Addison-Wesley.

Panman, R., & Panman, S. (2006). Group counseling and therapy. In J. L. Ronch, W. Van Ornum, & N. C. Stilwell (Eds.), *The counseling sourcebook.* New York: The Crossroad Publishing Company, pp. 44–59.

Posthuma, B. W. (2002). *Small groups in counseling and therapy: Process and leadership.* (4th ed.). Boston: Allyn and Bacon.

Prochaska, J. O., & DiClemente, C. C. (1982). Transtheoretical therapy: Toward a more integrative model of change. *Psychotherapy: Theory, Research and Practice, 19*, 276–288.

Purtilo, R., & Haddad, A. (2002). *Health professional and patient interaction* (6ᵗʰ ed.). Philadelphia: W.B. Saunders.

Seligman, M.E.P. (2002). *Authentic happiness: Using the new positive psychology to realize your potential for lasting fulfillment.* New York: Free Press.

Seligman, M.E.P. (1975). *Helplessness: On depression, development, and death.* San Francisco: Freeman.

Simpson, S., & Yoshioka, C. (1992). Aristotelian view of leisure: An outdoor recreation perspective. *Leisure Studies, 11*(3), 219 – 231.

Schoel, J., Prouty, D., & Radcliffe, P. (1988). *Islands of healing: A guide to adventure-based counseling.* Hamilton, MA: Project Adventure.

Triplett, N. (1897). The dynamogenic factors in pacemaking and competition. *American Journal of Psychology, 9,* 507–533.

Rogers, C. R. (1961). *On becoming a person: A therapist's view of psychotherapy.* Boston: Houghton Mifflin.

Voelkl, J. E. (1986). Effects of institutionalization upon residents of extended care facilities. *Activities, Adaptation and Aging, 8,* 37–46.

Widmer, M. A., & Ellis, G. D. (1998). The Aristotelian good life model: Integration of values into therapeutic recreation service delivery. *Therapeutic Recreation Journal, 32*(4), 290 – 302.

Wilensky, H. L. (1964). The professionalization of everyone? *The American Journal of Sociology, 70*(2), 137–158.

World Health Organization. (1948). *WHO definition of health.* Geneva, Switzerland: Author.

Zajonc, R.B. (1965). Social facilitation. *Science, 149,* 269 – 274.

About the Author

DAVID R. AUSTIN, Ph.D., FALS, FDRT, has 45 years of experience in recreational therapy as a practitioner and educator. Dr. Austin is the author of over 100 articles and several textbooks, including the widely used book, *Therapeutic Recreation: Processes and Techniques,* now in its sixth edition. He is the developer of one of the leading conceptual models in recreational therapy, the Health Protection/Health Promotion Model. He is a Fellow of both the Academy of Leisure Sciences and the National Academy of Recreational Therapists. Dr. Austin is the only individual to have received the NTRS Distinguished Service Award, the ATRA Distinguished Fellow Award, and the SPRE Distinguished Fellow Award. He has been named to the Union College Hall of Fame, was presented the Brightbill Award by the University of Illinois, and received the NRPA Literary Award. He counts as his greatest achievement being awarded Indiana University's highest teaching award, the Frederic Bachman Lieber Memorial Award for Distinguished Teaching.